The Umberto Menghi Cookbook

by
Umberto Menghi

with John Bishop
& Marian Babchuk

Talonbooks · Vancouver · 1982

Talonbooks
201 1019 East Cordova
Vancouver
British Columbia V6A 1M8
Canada

This book was typeset by Mary Schendlinger and David Lach at Baseline, designed by David Robinson and printed by Hemlock Printers Ltd. for Talonbooks. Colour separations by Tri Scan Graphics Ltd.

The text photographs were taken by Thomas Hayes.

Sixth printing: December 1988

Printed in Canada

Canadian Cataloguing in Publication Data

Menghi, Umberto, 1946-
    The Umberto Menghi cookbook

    Includes index.
    ISBN 0-88922-197-9

    1. Cookery, Italian.   I. Bishop, John,
1944-   II. Babchuk, Marian, 1954-
III. Title.
TX723.M46   641'.5945   C82-091308-1

to all my customers
for their support & encouragement
through the years

Table of Contents

Spaghetti alla Contadina/Spaghetti with Tomatoes and Peppers / 43
Spaghetti Amatriciana/Spaghetti with Tomatoes, Onion, Bacon and Cheese / 44
Spaghetti Bolognese/Spaghetti with Meat Sauce
and Spaghetti Caponata/Spaghetti with Eggplant, Zucchini, Peppers and Tomatoes / 45
Spaghetti Carbonara/Spaghetti with Ham, Eggs and Cream / 46
Spaghetti con Calamari/Spaghetti with Squid / 47
Spaghetti con Fegatini di Pollo/Spaghetti with Chicken Livers
and Spaghetti con Tonno/Spaghetti with Tuna / 48
Spaghetti Frutti di Mare/Spaghetti with Seafood / 49
Spaghetti Marinara/Spaghetti with Clams and Tomatoes / 50
Linguine al Pesto/Linguine with Pesto / 51
Linguine alle Vongole/Linguine with Clam Sauce / 52
Linguine con Cozze/Linguine with Mussels / 53
Linguine Gorgonzola/Linguine with Gorgonzola Cheese
and Fettuccine al Burro/Fettuccine with Butter / 54
Fettuccine alla Crema/Fettuccine with Cream
and Fettuccine alla Noce/Fettuccine with Walnuts / 55
Fettuccine con Animelle/Fettuccine with Sweetbreads / 56
Fettuccine con Asparagi/Fettuccine with Asparagus / 57
Fettuccine con Carciofi/Fettuccine with Artichokes
and Fettuccine con Caviale/Fettuccine with Caviar / 58
Fettuccine con Gamberetti/Fettuccine with Shrimp / 59
Fettuccine con Melanzane/Fettuccine with Eggplant / 60
Fettuccine con Porri/Fettuccine with Leeks / 61
Fettuccine con Prosciutto e Piselli/Fettuccine with Prosciutto and Peas
and Fettuccine con Quattro Formaggio/Fettuccine with Four Cheeses / 62
Fettuccine con Zucchini/Fettuccine with Zucchini / 63
Fettuccine Primavera/Fettuccine with Fresh Vegetables / 64
Fettuccine Scaloppate/Fettuccine with Scallops
and Fettuccine Verde alla Crema/Spinach Fettuccine in Cream / 65
Fettuccine Verde con Patate/Spinach Fettuccine with Potatoes / 66
Pasticcio di Rigatoni/Rigatoni Baked with Cream and Cheese / 67
Rigatoni al Peperoncino Rosso/Rigatoni with Red Peppers / 68
Rigatoni con Acciughe/Rigatoni with Anchovies
and Rigatoni Conchiglie di Mare/Rigatoni with Scallops / 71
Rigatoni del Caminetto/Rigatoni with Parsley, Garlic Butter, Italian Sausage and Red Peppers / 72
Rigatoni dell' Ortolano/Cold Vegetable and Herb Rigatoni / 73
Farfalle Salmonate/Pasta Bows with Salmon / 74
Farfalle con Rognoncini al Funghetto/Pasta Bows with Kidneys and Mushrooms
and Lumache con Tacchino e Piselli/Lumache with Turkey and Peas / 75
Tortellini alla Panna/Tortellini with Cream Sauce / 76
Tortellini Bolognese/Tortellini with Meat Sauce / 77
Tortellini Napoletana/Tortellini with Tomatoes
and Agnolotti con Ricotta e Spinaci/Agnolotti Stuffed with Ricotta Cheese and Spinach / 78
Agnolotti con Ripieno di Carne/Agnolotti Stuffed with Meat / 80
Cannelloni di Mare/Cannelloni Stuffed with Seafood and Spinach / 81
Cannelloni alla Fiorentina/Cannelloni Stuffed with Meat and Spinach / 82
Lasagna al Forno/Baked Lasagna / 84
Gnocchi alla Piemontese/Potato Dumplings with Meat Sauce / 85

PIATTI FORTI/MAIN COURSES

Main Courses / 86

SHELLFISH

Zuppa di Vongole all' Italiana/Steamed Clams in White Wine and Tomatoes / 89
Cozze Marinara/Mussels in White Wine, Cream and Onions / 90
Ostriche alla Fiorentina/Oysters Florentine / 91
Gamberoni Affinochiati/Prawns with Anise / 92
Scampi alla Griglia/Broiled Baby Lobster Tail / 93
Granchio alla Veneziana/Crab Stuffed with Shrimp and Spinach / 94
Alaska King Crab Legs Viareggio/Alaska King Crab Legs in Bernaise Sauce / 96
Granchio Mousseline/Crab Mousseline / 98
Calamari Fritti/Pan Fried Squid / 100
Calamari Ripieni/Stuffed Squid / 101

FISH

Sogliola al Vino Rosso/Sole in Red Wine Sauce / 102
Filetti di Sogliola al Vino Bianco con Crema/
Fillet of Sole in White Wine, Cream, Mushrooms and Tomatoes / 103
Sogliola alla Mugnaia/Dover Sole in Lemon Butter / 104
Cod Pizzaiola/Cod with Tomatoes, Garlic and Basil / 107
Halibut alla Genovese/Halibut in a Light Green Sauce / 108
Halibut Napoletana/Halibut with a Purée of Tomatoes and Clams / 109
Red Snapper al Vino Rosso/Red Snapper in Red Wine with Abalone / 110
Storgione della Cantina/Sturgeon with Avocado / 111
Grilse al Burro Bianco/Baby Salmon in Burro Bianco / 112
Salmone Affinochiato/Salmon in Fennel Sauce / 113
Salmone Cetriolato/Salmon with Cucumber / 114
Salmone con Acciughe/Salmon with Anchovy Sauce / 115
Cioppino/Fish Stew / 116

MEAT, FOWL & GAME

Filetto di Pollo al Barolo/Chicken Breasts in Red Wine Sauce / 118
Pollo con Prosciutto e Formaggio/Chicken with Prosciutto and Cheese / 119
Pollo con Zucchini Fritti/Breast of Chicken with Sautéed Zucchini / 120
Pollo Contadina/Chicken Stewed in Tomatoes, Red Wine, Onion and Peppers / 121
Pollo Diavolo/Grilled Chicken with Mustard Sauce / 122
Pollo Oreganato al Limone/Chicken with Oregano and Lemon / 125
Pollo Zafferato/Breast of Chicken in Cream with Saffron / 126
Gallinella con Frutta di Stagione/Cornish Game Hen Stuffed with Fruit / 127
Faraona in Umido/Guinea Hen with Smoked Bacon / 128
Quaglie con Uva e Brandy/Quail with Grape and Brandy Sauce / 130
Pernice Ripiena Arrostita/Partridge Stuffed with Wild Rice / 131
Anitra all' Arancio/Duck with Orange Sauce / 133
Anitra con Cedro/Duck with Honey and Lime Sauce / 135
Fagiano con Funghi e Champagne/Pheasant with Mushrooms and Champagne Sauce / 136
Tacchino Ripieno con Salsicce e Castagne/Turkey Stuffed with Sausage and Chestnut / 138
Involtini di Tacchino/Turkey with Belgian Endive Pizzaiola / 141
Oca Farcita Bongustaio/Roast Stuffed Goose / 142
Coniglio Arrosto/Roast Rabbit
and Filetto di Capriolo Pepato/Reindeer Steak with Pepper and Brandy Sauce / 144
Animelle di Vitello/Sweetbreads / 145
Medaglione di Vitello Boscaiolo/Medallions of Veal in Mushroom Sauce / 146
Nodino di Vitello all' Aglio/Fillet of Veal with Garlic Sauce / 147
Scaloppine al Limone/Veal Scallops in Lemon Sauce / 148
Scaloppine al Marsala/Veal Scallops in Marsala Wine / 149

VEGETABLES

DESSERTS

INDEX

Introduction

Umberto Menghi was born in 1946 in Florence, Italy, a city well-known for its art, literature, architecture, politics and cuisine. Food has always fascinated Umberto. As a child, he spent so much time at the *trattoria* next door to his parents' house that the owners, in self-defence, finally were forced to give him a job. Umberto also remembers secret excursions up a ladder to the *granaio*, a space between the first and second floors in Florentine houses where food is stored. To this day, in each of Umberto's restaurants, there is a staircase (sometimes leading nowhere). To Umberto, a staircase means food and a full stomach!

The Umberto Menghi Cookbook comes from a man who knows food well and who knows how to cook it. By the time Umberto was fifteen years old, he had decided to make the preparation and service of food his life's work. At fifteen, he applied to hotel and restaurant management school in Rome and was accepted, taking their three-year course. After graduation, Umberto worked waiting tables and cooking in Italy, France, Jersey and England. He came to Canada in 1967, for Expo '67, where he worked at the Queen Elizabeth Hotel in Montreal. In 1969, he bought a one-way train ticket to Vancouver. He liked the setting of Vancouver very much and discovered that people there were receptive to his ideas. Surveying the restaurant scene, he found that Italian restaurants in Vancouver were stereotyped —red checkered tablecloths and spaghetti and meatballs. Obviously what was needed was a new style of Italian restaurant! Umberto opened his first restaurant in Vancouver in 1972. In 1973, at the age of twenty-seven, he opened Umberto's in the old yellow house on Hornby Street. Vancouver hasn't been the same since!

Umberto's on Hornby Street was an overnight success. On the night it opened, Umberto served veal, veal and veal! If a customer wanted a bottle of wine, Umberto would ask for the money up front and dash out the back door to fetch the bottle! The high demand for reservations and the common complaint that Vancouver did not have a good seafood restaurant led to plans for expansion. Rather than expand the menu at Umberto's ("Why change a good thing?" asks Umberto), Umberto waited for the building next door to become available—and la Cantina was born. Next, on the other side of the old yellow house, Umberto built Il Giardino. Il Giardino is modelled after a Tuscan villa and serves meat, game and fowl, three of the staples of a Florentine diet. Il Palazzo, with its classic Florentine cooking, followed Il Giardino. Vancouver was turning into a "restaurant city"; people were beginning to go out during the week, not waiting to go out on the weekends. Umberto al Porto, in Gastown, was Umberto's next venture. He wanted to broaden his base, so with Umberto al Porto, he created a restaurant with a casual atmosphere, a restaurant where you did not have to wait to get in, where you could bring your friends and have an inexpensive good meal—pasta ("The food of the future," Umberto says) and salad, or a main course; dessert and coffee. Il Caminetto at

Whistler Mountain Ski Village opened in 1982—and soon, using the al Porto model, Umberto will have restaurants in Seattle (Fall 1982) and San Francisco (1983).

What Umberto Menghi represents in his restaurants is quality. "It is something," Umberto says, "I will never sacrifice"; it is something that will never go out of style; and, given the choice, it is something that people will always desire. This is Umberto Menghi's philosophy. It is a philosophy that is apparent in all of his restaurants—and that is featured in this book, *The Umberto Menghi Cookbook*. All of the recipes in this book have been drawn from the menus of Umberto's six superior restaurants. There are 159 recipes in all—everything from antipasto to zabaglione.

What Umberto Menghi has done in his life is move Italian cooking through the places he has lived—from Florence, which is in Tuscany in Northern Italy, through the rest of Italy, through France, through England to North America. In Italy, food is not imported; everything available is used. Everything is simple and fresh. That is what Italian cooking is all about and that is what this cookbook is all about—using the best fresh available ingredients to prepare the best food.

The recipes in this book are straightforward and easy to prepare. "When your guests come for dinner," Umberto says, "they don't want you to spend all your time in the kitchen. They want to see *you!*" And so they will, for most of the recipes in this book can be prepared in less than one-half hour.

When asked about *The Umberto Menghi Cookbook*—how to describe it; what to tell people about the book—Umberto replies with a laugh and a boast: "Just tell people that it's the best Italian cookbook this side of the Atlantic!" And so it is!

Feast your eyes and your appetites on this book!

Vancouver, B.C.
July, 1982.

Antipasto

Antipasto are hors d'oeuvres or appetizers. Quite literally, the word *antipasto* means "before the meal." It is something you serve to stimulate the appetite. That is its function, first and foremost.

You can eat antipasto at a table, with a knife and fork, or you can serve it on a tray to guests as canapés about one hour before the meal. What you serve as an antipasto depends on your menu and on the season. Antipasto is always light—just a taste. It is whatever you have in the house—anything you have that is handy or readily available; whatever you have in your garden or your refrigerator. It is something you can serve quickly and easily. It could be: cheese, olives, eggs; vegetables (raw—mixed fresh vegetables; marinated—like mushroom caps or artichoke hearts; or cooked—like *caponata*, which is zucchini, eggplant, peppers and tomatoes in a casserole; or *peperonata*, which are braised sweet peppers; or *fagioli con olio*, which are cooked white kidney beans); small fish such as smelts or sardines; fresh *frutti di mare*, such as shrimp, prawns or squid, or pickled herring; pâté, or *affettati*, which are cold cuts such as carpaccio, prosciutto, salami, mortadella.

The important thing with antipasto is to coordinate it to your menu. You wouldn't have Prosciutto con Melone, for instance, if you were serving Fettuccine con Prosciutto e Piselli. Antipasto should balance your meal, counterpoint it—lead into the meal. There is really no recipe for antipasto. We have illustrated a plate of antipasto on page 17 (please study this illustration); and on pages 12-16, we have written out recipes for five items that you may serve as antipasto. For the recipes for *caponata* and *peperonata*, please see the Vegetable section.

LUMACHE ALL' AGLIO
Snails in Garlic Sauce

Pre-heat oven to 400° F/200° C.

1 1/2 (4 1/2 oz./125 g.) cans of
Burgundy snails, drained
(36 snails)

Wash snail shells carefully.

36 snail shells

Garlic Butter:

2/3 cup/150 g. butter, softened
1 small shallot, finely chopped
6 cloves garlic, finely chopped
4 tbsp./60 g. fresh parsley,
finely chopped
1 tbsp./15 mL. dry white vermouth
juice of 1/2 lemon
1 tsp./5 g. salt
freshly ground black pepper (to taste)

Mix softened butter, shallot, garlic, parsley, vermouth, lemon juice, salt and pepper together in a bowl.

Put snails in shells and cover each snail with 1 tsp./5 g. of garlic butter.

Put shells on a baking sheet or in snail dishes in oven and bake at 400° F/200° C for 10-15 minutes until butter is bubbling.

This recipe for Lumache all' Aglio serves 6 people. The shells can be stuffed ahead of time and frozen. Serve with slices of crusty bread.

CONCHIGLIE CON BASILICO
Scallops with Basil and White Wine

8 oz./250 g. fresh scallops salt (to taste) freshly ground black pepper (to taste)	*Season scallops with salt and pepper.*
1 tsp./5 mL. olive oil 1 tsp./5 g. butter	*Sauté scallops and garlic in oil and butter in a skillet on medium heat for 3 minutes, stirring frequently (2-3 minutes longer if scallops are large; high heat if scallops were previously frozen).*
1/8 tsp./pinch of garlic, finely chopped	*Add garlic to scallops and sauté on medium heat for another 2 minutes. Remove scallops from skillet and keep warm.*

Sauce:

3/4 cup/175 mL. fish stock (see p. 30) 2 tbsp./30 mL. dry white wine	*Mix fish stock and wine together in a skillet and reduce by simmering on medium heat for 2-3 minutes until fish stock thickens slightly and becomes velvety.*
juice of 1/2 lemon 2 tsp./10 g. fresh basil, finely chopped	*Add lemon juice and basil to fish stock and wine and stir until well blended.*
2 tbsp./30 mL. whipping cream	*Add cream to fish stock, wine, lemon juice and basil and stir until well blended.*
salt (to taste) freshly ground black pepper (to taste)	*Season with salt and pepper.*
	Add scallops to sauce and simmer on medium heat for approximately 1 minute.
1/2 lemon, cut in wedges	*Put scallops on a warm serving platter or on warm plates. Coat with sauce, garnish with lemon wedges and serve.*

This recipe for Conchiglie con Basilico serves 2 people.

CARPACCIO
Marinated Raw Fillet of Beef

5 oz./150 g. lean fillet of beef

Put fillet of beef in freezer until it firms up, then slice paper thin using a slicing machine — or have your butcher slice beef paper thin.

Marinade:

2 tsp./10 mL. lemon juice
2 tsp./10 g. Dijon mustard
salt (to taste)
freshly ground black pepper (to taste)

Mix lemon juice, mustard, salt and pepper together in a bowl.

2 tsp./10 mL. olive oil

Slowly add oil to lemon juice, mustard, salt and pepper and whisk constantly in the same direction until oil is well blended.

Pour marinade over slices of beef and refrigerate for at least 30 minutes.

freshly ground black pepper (to taste)

Serve with freshly ground black pepper.

This recipe for Carpaccio serves 2 people. Serve with toasted bread.

PROSCIUTTO CON MELONE
Prosciutto with Melon

1/2 honeydew melon or cantaloupe, sliced lengthwise in four

Slice melon or cantaloupe 1/2-1 inch/ 1-2.5 cm. from each end between melon and rind.

Put melon or canteloupe on salad plates.

2-3 oz./50-85 g. prosciutto, sliced paper thin

Lay 2 slices of prosciutto over each piece of melon or canteloupe.

freshly ground black pepper (to taste)

Grind pepper over prosciutto slices and serve.

This recipe for Prosciutto con Melone serves 2 people. Prosciutto is illustrated at the back of the antipasto photograph on p. 17.

PATE
Pâté

Pre-heat oven to 325° F/160° C.

8 oz./250 g. pork fat, diced
8 oz./250 g. veal stew or trim, diced
8 oz./250 g. boneless chicken leg, diced
8 oz./250 g. chicken livers, diced
2 cloves garlic, finely chopped

Grind pork fat, veal stew or trim, chicken, chicken livers and garlic in a grinder or food processor.

2 eggs
2 tbsp./30 mL. brandy
2 tbsp./30 mL. Madeira wine
1 tsp./5 g. fresh thyme, crushed
1/8 tsp./pinch of fresh basil, crushed
1 tsp./5 g. salt
1 tbsp./15 g. green Madagascar peppercorns

Beat eggs in a bowl, then add brandy, wine, thyme, basil, salt and peppercorns and mix together.

Add eggs, brandy, wine, thyme, basil, salt and peppercorns to pork fat, veal stew or trim, chicken, chicken livers and garlic and mix together thoroughly.

2 oz./50 g. raw bacon
(2 strips)

Line the bottom of a 10 x 3 x 3 inch/ 25 x 8 x 8 cm. ovenproof ceramic dish or meatloaf tin with strips of bacon.

Fill half of the ceramic dish or meatloaf tin with pâté mixture.

2 rabbit livers or chicken livers

Place rabbit livers or chicken livers in a line down the centre of the pâté mixture.

Fill up dish or tin with the remaining pâté mixture and cover with aluminum foil.

cold water

Put dish or tin in a roasting pan filled with enough water to cover two-thirds of the mold.

*Put roasting pan in oven and bake at 325° F/160° C for 2 hours.
Set dish or tin aside to cool, then refrigerate for 1-2 days to allow pâté to set.*

This recipe for Pâté serves 10-15 people. Serve with toast and sweet gherkins.

Illustration #1: Antipasto. *On the tray in the foreground (from the outer edge):* rolled slices of Mozzarella cheese and salami, black olives, artichoke hearts, *peperonata* (braised red and green sweet peppers) interspersed with stuffed squid, sautéed slices of eggplant, *fagioli con olio* (cooked white kidney beans) garnished with rolled anchovy fillets. *In the background (at the left):* salami and prosciutto. Tiles courtesy of World Mosaic Ltd.

Soups

CONSOMME DI POLLO
Chicken Consommé

1 chicken carcass	*Chop chicken carcass into large pieces and put into a pot.*
1 small onion, ground 1 small carrot, ground 1 stalk celery, ground	*Add onion, carrot and celery to chicken carcass.*
3 quarts/3 L. cold water	*Cover chicken carcass, onion, carrot and celery with water and bring to a boil on high heat, frequently skimming the froth off the top.*
1 bayleaf 1/8 tsp./pinch of thyme salt (to taste) white pepper (to taste)	*Season with bayleaf, thyme, salt and pepper (but use less salt and pepper than you normally would; reduction will make the consommé saltier) and reduce by simmering on very low heat for 2-3 hours.*
	Carefully strain consommé through a sieve lined with a linen or muslin cloth.

This recipe for Consommé di Pollo yields approximately 8 cups/2 L.. Chicken consommé is used in many of the recipes in this book, so make it ahead and keep it in a sealed plastic container in your refrigerator or freeze it in ice cube trays so that you have it on hand and can use it whenever required. It can be kept in your refrigerator for up to 2 weeks.

Illustration #2: Soup. *From left to right:* Minestrone alla Toscana, Zuppa di Pesce and Stracciatella alla Romana. Tiles courtesy of World Mosaic Ltd.; shell-shaped bowl courtesy of The Patio Gallery; serviettes courtesy of Georg Jensen.

CONSOMME DI MANZO
Beef Consommé

1 beef knuckle bone with a little meat on the bone or equivalent weight of soup bones with meat on	Chop knuckle bone or soup bones into large pieces and put into a pot.
1 large onion, halved 1 small carrot, ground 1 stalk celery, ground 1 small leek, ground	Add onion, carrot, celery and leek to knuckle bone or soup bones.
3 quarts/3 L. cold water	Cover knuckle bone or soup bones, onion, carrot, celery and leek with water and bring to a boil on high heat, frequently skimming the froth off the top.
1 bayleaf 1/8 tsp./pinch of sage 1/8 tsp./pinch of thyme	Season with bayleaf, sage and thyme (but no salt and pepper yet) and reduce by simmering on very low heat for 2-3 hours.
	Carefully strain consommé through a sieve lined with a linen or muslin cloth.
salt (to taste) white pepper (to taste)	Season with salt and pepper.

This recipe for Consommé di Manzo yields approximately 8 cups/2 L.. Beef consommé is used in many of the recipes in this book, so make it ahead and keep it in a sealed plastic container in your refrigerator or freeze it in ice cube trays so that you have it on hand and can use it whenever required. It can be kept in your refrigerator for up to 2 weeks.

STRACCIATELLA ALLA ROMANA
Chicken Soup with Eggs and Parsley

4-6 cups/900 mL.-1.5 L. chicken consommé (*see p. 19*)

Put chicken consommé in a pot and bring to a boil on high heat.

Egg Mixture:

4 eggs
1/3 cup/75 g. Parmesan cheese, coarsely grated
juice of 1/2 lemon
1 tbsp./15 g. fresh parsley, finely chopped

Beat eggs in a bowl, then add Parmesan cheese, lemon juice and parsley and mix together.

Remove chicken consommé from heat, but leave in pot.

Add egg mixture to chicken consommé and stir.

Return chicken consommé and egg mixture to medium heat and simmer for 2-3 minutes, stirring frequently.

Pour soup into warm soup bowls, stirring while soup is being poured so that egg is evenly distributed throughout chicken consommé, and serve.

This recipe for Stracciatella alla Romana serves 6 people. Stracciatella alla Romana is illustrated on p. 18.

MINESTRONE ALLA TOSCANA
Tuscany Style Vegetable Soup

2 tbsp./30 mL. olive oil 1 cup/250 g. tomato, diced 1 cup/250 g. onion, finely chopped 1 cup/250 g. carrot, diced 1/2 cup/125 g. celery, diced 1/2 cup/125 g. zucchini, diced 1/2 cup/125 g. eggplant, diced 3 cloves garlic, finely chopped	*Sauté tomato, onion, carrot, celery, zucchini, eggplant and garlic in oil in a deep soup pot on medium heat for 10 minutes.*
8 oz./250 g. ground beef or ground veal	*Add ground beef or ground veal to tomato, onion, carrot, celery, zucchini, eggplant and garlic and sauté on medium heat for another 5 minutes.*
10 cups/2.5 L. cold water 1 tbsp./15 mL. tomato paste 1 tsp./5 g. oregano salt (to taste) freshly ground black pepper (to taste)	*Add water, tomato paste, oregano, salt and pepper to tomato, onion, carrot, celery, zucchini, eggplant, garlic and ground beef or ground veal and slowly bring to a boil on medium heat, stirring constantly, then simmer on low heat for 30 minutes.*
1/2 cup/125 g. cooked white kidney beans 1/2 cup/125 g. potato, peeled and diced	*Add kidney beans and potato to tomato, onion, carrot, celery, zucchini, eggplant, garlic, ground beef or ground veal, water, tomato paste, oregano, salt and pepper and simmer on low heat for another 10 minutes until potato is cooked.*
	Ladle soup into a warm soup tureen or into warm soup bowls.
1/3 cup/75 g. Parmesan cheese, coarsely grated 6 tsp./30 g. fresh parsley, finely chopped	*Sprinkle with Parmesan cheese and parsley and serve.*

This recipe for Minestrone alla Toscana serves 6 people. Once cooked, it can be refrigerated for 1 week and warmed up as necessary. If the consistency is too thick, just add water. Add salt and pepper to taste before serving. Minestrone alla Toscana is illustrated on p. 18.

ZUPPA DI CAVOLO
Cauliflower Soup

1 head of cauilflower, finely chopped, reserving 1/4 head for garnish
2 large potatoes, peeled and quartered

Put cauliflower and potatoes in a deep soup pot.

1 cup/250 mL. cold water

Add water to pot, then cover pot, bring to a boil on high heat and steam cauliflower and potatoes until they are very well cooked, careful not to burn them, then drain.

4 cups/900 mL. whipping cream
2 cups/450 mL. half and half cream

Add whipping cream and half and half cream to cauliflower and potatoes in pot and slowly bring to a boil on medium heat, stirring constantly, then simmer on low heat for 30 minutes.

Carefully strain soup into another soup pot through a sieve lined with a linen or muslin cloth and return to medium heat. Discard cauliflower and potatoes.

salt (to taste)
freshly ground black pepper (to taste)

Season with salt and pepper.

1/4 head of cauliflower, finely chopped (for garnish)

Add raw cauliflower to soup, then ladle soup into ovenproof soup bowls.

3/4 cup/175 g. Parmesan cheese, coarsely grated

Sprinkle with Parmesan cheese.

Put soup bowls in oven, broil until cheese is golden and serve.

This recipe for Zuppa di Cavolo serves 6 people.

ZUPPA DI OSTRICHE
Oyster Soup

12 oz./350 g. fresh oysters	Scrape black from oysters and cut oysters in half.
2 tsp./10 g. butter 1 small onion, diced medium 2 small cloves garlic, finely chopped	Sauté onion and garlic in butter in a deep soup pot on medium heat until onion is transparent, careful not to burn the garlic.
1 medium ripe tomato	Blanch tomato by dropping it into a saucepan of boiling water until skin splits. Peel, seed and chop tomato. Add tomato to onion and garlic.
1/2 lemon, peeled, skinned and diced medium	Add lemon to onion, garlic and tomato and mix together.
1 cup/250 mL. dry white wine	Add wine to onion, garlic, tomato and lemon and reduce by one-half by simmering on low heat for approximately 10 minutes.
	Add oysters to onion, garlic, tomato, lemon and wine.
2 cups/450 mL. white sauce (see p. 32), thin consistency	Gradually add white sauce to onion, garlic, tomato, lemon, wine and oysters and stir until smoooth.
2 cups/450 mL. whipping cream	Gradually add cream to onion, garlic, tomato, lemon, wine, oysters and white sauce and stir until well blended, then simmer on low heat until soup is thick enough to coat the back of a spoon.
1/8 tsp./pinch of basil 1/8 tsp./pinch of thyme a dash of tabasco sauce a dash of Worcestershire sauce salt (to taste) freshly ground black pepper (to taste)	Add basil, thyme, tabasco sauce and Worcestershire sauce to soup, then season with salt and pepper.
	Ladle soup into a warm soup tureen or into warm soup bowls.
3 tsp./15 g. fresh parsley, finely chopped	Sprinkle with parsley and serve.

This recipe for Zuppa di Ostriche serves 6 people.

ZUPPA DI PESCE
Fish Soup

1/4 cup/50 mL. olive oil
1 lb./450 g. fish bones,
coarsely chopped
1 small onion, finely chopped
1 stalk celery and celery top,
finely chopped
1 leek, washed and finely chopped
2 tbsp./30 mL. tomato paste

Sauté fish bones, onion, celery and leek in oil in a deep soup pot on high heat for approximately 5 minutes, then add tomato paste, stir until well blended and simmer on high heat for another 1-2 minutes.

1/2 cup/125 mL. dry white wine

Deglaze soup pot with wine and reduce by simmering on high heat for 1-2 minutes.

2 quarts/2 L. cold water
1 bunch of fresh parsley stalks
1 bayleaf

Add water, parsley stalks and bayleaf to fish bones, onion, celery, leek, tomato paste and wine and slowly bring to a boil on medium heat, then simmer on low heat for 30-40 minutes.

Carefully strain soup into another soup pot through a sieve lined with a linen or muslin cloth and return to low heat.

1 1/2 tbsp./20 g. butter,
slightly softened
1 tbsp./15 g. flour

Mix butter and flour together in a saucepan on medium heat, stirring constantly, to make a roux, then add roux, bit by bit, to soup in pot, stir until well blended and simmer on low heat for at least 5 minutes.

2 tbsp./30 mL. olive oil
4 oz./125 g. fresh scallops
4 oz./125 g. fillet of salmon,
cut in small pieces
4 oz./125 g. fillet of red snapper,
cut in small pieces

Sauté scallops, salmon and red snapper in hot oil in a skillet on high heat for 4-5 minutes.

2 tbsp./30 mL. Pernod

Deglaze skillet with Pernod.

Add scallops, salmon and red snapper to soup and gently poach on medium heat for 10-15 minutes until fish is just done.

Ladle soup into a warm soup tureen or into warm soup bowls.

6 tsp./30 mL. whipping cream

Garnish with cream and serve.

This recipe for Zuppa di Pesce serves 6 people. Zuppa di Pesce is illustrated on p. 18.

OLIO E ACETO
Oil and Vinegar Dressing

All ingredients must be at room temperature.

2 tbsp./30 mL. white wine vinegar
1 tbsp./15 g. Dijon mustard
2 cloves garlic, finely chopped
salt (to taste)
freshly ground black pepper (to taste)

Mix vinegar, mustard, garlic, salt and pepper together in a bowl.

1/2 cup/125 mL. olive oil

Slowly add oil in a steady stream to vinegar, mustard, salt and pepper and whisk constantly in the same direction until oil is well blended.

This recipe for Olio e Aceto yields approximately 3/4 cup/175 mL.. Use 1 tbsp./15 mL. per portion when serving with salads. This recipe can be used as a dressing for all types of salads and cold fresh vegetables. Use on top of fresh vegetables and serve as an antipasto.

CONDIMENTO DI ERBE
Herb Condiments

All ingredients must be at room temperature.

1 tbsp./15 g. Dijon mustard
1 tsp./5 g. fresh parsley, finely chopped
2 cloves garlic, finely chopped
1 tsp./5 g. fresh basil, finely chopped
1 tsp./5 g. fresh tarragon, finely chopped
1 tsp./5 g. fresh chervil, finely chopped

Mix mustard, parsley, garlic, basil, tarragon and chervil together in a bowl.

2 tbsp./30 mL. lemon juice
2 tbsp./30 mL. vinegar

Add lemon juice and vinegar to mustard, parsley, garlic, basil, tarragon and chervil and stir until well blended.

3/4 cup/175 mL. olive oil

Slowly add oil in a steady stream to mustard, parsley, garlic, basil, tarragon, chervil, lemon juice and vinegar and whisk constantly in the same direction until oil is well blended.

1 dash of tabasco sauce

Add tabasco sauce to mustard, parsley, garlic, basil, tarragon, chervil, lemon juice, vinegar and oil and stir until well blended.

salt (to taste)
freshly ground black pepper (to taste)

Season with salt and pepper.

This recipe for Condimento di Erbe yields approximately 1 cup/250 mL.. Use 1 tbsp./ 15 mL. per portion when serving with salads. This recipe can be used as a dresing for all types of salads and cold fresh vegetables. Use on top of fresh vegetables and serve as an antipasto.

INSALATA DI MARE
Butter Lettuce Salad with Marinated Fresh Scallops

4 oz./125 g. fresh mushrooms	*Wash mushrooms and dry them with a cloth or paper towel, then slice.*
4 oz./125 g. fresh scallops	*Pat scallops dry with a cloth or paper towel, then slice 1/2 inch/1 cm. thick.*
2 green onions, coarsely chopped (the entire onion)	
	Put mushrooms, scallops and onions together in a bowl.

Dressing:

juice of 1 lemon (approximately 1/3 cup/75 mL. lemon juice) 2 tbsp./30 mL. dry white wine 1 tbsp./15 g. Dijon mustard 2 cloves garlic, finely chopped 1 tbsp./15 g. fresh parsley, finely chopped salt (to taste) freshly ground black pepper (to taste)	*Mix lemon juice, wine, mustard, garlic, parsley, salt and pepper together in another bowl.*
1/2 cup/125 mL. olive oil	*Slowly add oil in a steady stream to lemon juice, wine, mustard, garlic, parsley, salt and pepper and whisk constantly in the same direction until oil is well blended.*
	Put mushrooms, scallops and onions in the bowl with dressing and toss together.
	Refrigerate for at least 2 hours.
1-2 heads of butter lettuce (depending on size)	*Wash and dry lettuce well.*
1 small ripe tomato, sliced 6-8 black Calamata olives	*Add tomato and olives to lettuce before serving, then add mushrooms, scallops, onions and dressing and toss together. Serve on salad plates.*

This recipe for Insalata di Mare serves 2 people.

INSALATA MISTA
Mixed Salad

1 head of butter lettuce 1 Belgian endive 1 tomato, quartered 1/2 stalk celery, julienned	*Wash and dry lettuce and endive well.* *Put lettuce, endive, tomato and celery* *in a bowl.*

Dressing:

a few drops of lemon juice 1 tbsp./15 mL. red wine vinegar 1 tsp./5 g. Dijon mustard 2 cloves garlic, finely chopped salt (to taste) freshly ground black pepper (to taste)	*Mix lemon juice, vinegar, mustard,* *garlic, salt and pepper together* *in another bowl.*
1/3 cup/75 mL. olive oil	*Slowly add oil in a steady stream* *to lemon juice, vinegar, mustard, garlic,* *salt and pepper and whisk constantly* *in the same direction until oil* *is well blended.*
1 tbsp./15 g. fresh parsley, finely chopped	*Pour dressing over lettuce, endive, tomato* *and celery and toss together.* *Sprinkle with parsley and serve* *on salad plates.*

This recipe for Insalata Mista serves 2 people.

INSALATA DI POMODORI CON BASILICO
Tomato Salad with Fresh Basil

2 medium ripe tomatoes, thinly sliced	*Arrange tomato slices on a serving platter* *or on salad plates.*
10-12 leaves of fresh basil	*Put 1 basil leaf on top of each tomato* *slice.*
salt (to taste) freshly ground black pepper (to taste)	*Sprinkle salt and pepper over tomato* *slices.*
1 tbsp./15 mL. red wine vinegar	*Sprinkle vinegar over tomato slices.*
2 tbsp./30 mL. olive oil	*Sprinkle olive oil over tomato slices* *and serve.*

This recipe for Insalata di Pomorodi con Basilico serves 2 people.

CONSOMME DI PESCE
Fish Stock

2 lbs./1 kg. white fish bones
and trimmings
1 large onion, diced large
1/2 stalk celery, diced large
3 stalks of fresh parsley
1 bayleaf
3/4 cup/175 mL. dry white wine

Put fish bones and trimmings, onion, celery, parsley, bayleaf and wine into a pot.

2 quarts/2 L. cold water
salt (to taste)
white pepper (to taste)

Cover fish bones and trimmings, onion, celery, parsley, bayleaf and wine with water, stir until well blended and bring to a boil on high heat, then reduce by simmering on low heat for 2 hours.

Carefully strain fish stock through a sieve lined with a linen or muslin cloth.

This recipe for Consommé di Pesce yields approximately 4 cups/900 mL.. Fish stock is used in many of the recipes in this book, so make it ahead and keep it in a sealed plastic container in your refrigerator or freeze it in ice cube trays in your freezer. It can be kept in the refrigerator for up to 2 weeks. If previously frozen, gently warm fish stock before using.

FONDO DI VITELLO
Veal Stock

Pre-heat oven to 400° F/200° C.

1 onion, diced large
1 carrot, diced large
1 stalk celery and celery top, diced large
2-3 stalks of fresh parsley, chopped
1 leek, washed and diced large (optional)

Put onion, carrot, celery, parsley and leek on the bottom of a casserole dish or roasting pan.

1 lb./450 g. veal bones
1 lb./450 g. veal trimmings

Cover onion, carrot, celery, parsley and leek with veal bones and veal trimmings.

1/2 cup/125 mL. cold water

Pour water over top of onion, carrot, celery, parsley, leek, veal bones and veal trimmings and put casserole dish or roasting pan in oven and bake at 400° F/200° C for 20 minutes until veal bones and trimmings are lightly browned.

1/2 cup/125 mL. oil
1/2 cup/125 g. flour

Mix oil and flour together in a pot on medium heat, stirring constantly, to make a roux.

Add onion, carrot, celery, parsley, leek, veal bones, veal trimmings and water to roux in pot and stir until well blended.

1/2 cup/125 mL. dry red wine

Add wine to onion, carrot, celery, parsley, leek, veal bones, veal trimmings, water and roux and stir until well blended.

1 bayleaf
1 bouquet garni

Season with bayleaf and bouquet garni.

3 quarts/3 L. cold water

Cover onion, carrot, celery, parsley, leek, veal bones, veal trimmings, water, roux, wine, bayleaf and bouquet garni with water and bring to a boil on high heat, then reduce by simmering on low heat for 1 1/2-2 hours, frequently skimming the froth and excess oil off the top.

Carefully strain veal stock through a sieve lined with a linen or muslin cloth.

This recipe for Fondo di Vitello yields 6-8 cups/1.5-2 L.. Veal stock is used in many of the recipes in this book, so make it ahead and keep it in a sealed plastic container in your refrigerator or freeze it in ice cube trays in your freezer. It can be kept in the refrigerator for up to 2 weeks. If previously frozen, gently warm veal stock before using. For demi-glace (see p. 170), reduce this veal stock recipe for 3-4 hours.

SALSA AIOLI
Garlic and Mayonnaise Sauce

All ingredients must be at room temperature.

3 egg yolks	*Beat egg yolks in a deep bowl with a whisk until they become lemon-coloured.*
1 tbsp./15 mL. lemon juice 1 tbsp./15 mL. red wine vinegar 6 cloves garlic, finely chopped salt (to taste) freshly ground black pepper (to taste)	*Add lemon juice, vinegar, garlic, salt and pepper to egg yolks and stir until well blended.*
2 cups/450 mL. olive oil	*Slowly add oil in a steady stream to egg yolks, lemon juice, vinegar, garlic, salt and pepper and whisk constantly in the same direction until oil is well blended.*

This recipe for Salsa Aioli yields approximately 2 cups/450 mL.. Serve this sauce with Coniglio Arrosto (see p. 144).

SALSA BIANCA
White Sauce

2 tbsp./30 g. butter 2 tbsp./30 g. flour	*Melt butter in a saucepan on medium heat, then add flour and simmer on low heat for 2-3 minutes, whisking constantly.*
1 cup/250 mL. milk 1 cup/250 mL. half and half cream	*Add milk and half and half cream to butter and flour and simmer on low heat, whisking frequently, until sauce thickens.*
salt (to taste) white pepper (to taste) 1/8 tsp./pinch of nutmeg	*Season with salt, pepper and nutmeg.*

This recipe for Salsa Bianca yields 1 3/4 cups/400 mL.. White sauce is used in many of the recipes in this book.

SALSA DI POMODORO
Tomato Sauce

1 tbsp./15 mL. olive oil
1 tbsp./15 g. butter
1 large onion, finely chopped

Sauté onion in oil and butter in a pot on medium heat until onion is transparent.

1 medium carrot, finely chopped
1 stalk celery, finely chopped

Add carrot and celery to onion and sauté on medium heat for approximately 5 minutes.

2 (28 oz./796 mL.) cans of peeled Italian tomatoes, finely chopped, and their liquid
2 tbsp./30 mL. tomato paste
4 cloves garlic, minced
1 bayleaf
1 tsp./5 g. fresh oregano
1/2 tsp./2 g. fresh basil
1 whole clove, crushed
1 tbsp./15 g. sugar
1/2 cup/125 mL. dry red wine

Add tomatoes and their liquid, tomato paste, garlic, bayleaf, oregano, basil, cloves, sugar and wine to onion, carrot and celery and bring to a boil on high heat, stirring frequently, then simmer, uncovered, on low heat for 1 hour.

salt (to taste)
freshly ground black pepper (to taste)

Season with salt and pepper.

Strain sauce through a fine sieve. This should be a rich, thick sauce — if sauce is too thin after straining, continue to simmer on low heat; if sauce is too thick, add a little water.

1 tbsp./15 mL. olive oil

When sauce has reached desired consistency, remove from heat and add oil on top, but do not mix in.

Allow sauce to cool, uncovered and unrefrigerated, for at least 4 hours.

This recipe for Salsa di Pomodoro yields approximately 6 cups/1.5 L.. Tomato sauce is used in many of the recipes in this book, so make it ahead and keep it in a sealed plastic container in your refrigerator. It can be refrigerated for up to 2 weeks.

SALSA DI CARNE
Meat Sauce

1/4 cup/50 mL. olive oil 1 large onion, chopped	*Sauté onion in oil in a large skillet on medium heat until onion is transparent.*
1 lb./450 g. lean ground beef 4 cloves garlic, chopped	*Add ground beef and garlic to onion and sauté on medium heat for approximately 5 minutes until ground beef is evenly brown.*
6 large ripe tomatoes, finely chopped	*Add tomatoes to onion, ground beef and garlic.*
2 tbsp./30 mL. tomato paste 1 cup/250 mL. dry red wine 1 cup/250 mL. beef consommé (see p. 20) 2 bayleaves salt (to taste) freshly ground black pepper (to taste)	*Add tomato paste, wine, beef consommé, bayleaves, salt and pepper to onion, ground beef, garlic and tomatoes, stir until well blended and cook, uncovered, on low heat for 1 hour, stirring frequently.*

This recipe for Meat Sauce yields approximately 6 cups/1.5 L.. It can be refrigerated in a sealed plastic container for up to 2 weeks. This meat sauce is used in Spaghetti Bolognese, Lasagna al Forno, Agnolotti con Ripieno di Carne and Tortellini Bolognese.

Illustration #3: Pasta Still Life. *From left to right:* gnocchi, rigatoni, fresh spaghetti (*foreground*), fresh fettuccine verde, fresh fettuccine all' uvo, lumache, spaghettini (*in the clay dish*), spaghetti, farfalle and tortellini. *On top of the Parmesan cheese:* fresh pasta strips for cannelloni or lasagna. Studio: Thomas Hayes.

Pasta

Pasta comes in all shapes and sizes. In this book, there is: spaghettini (thin spaghetti), spaghetti (which is round, thin and long), linguine (which is flatter and broader than spaghetti), fettuccine (which is about 1/4 inch/.5 cm. wide, flat and long; and which comes as egg noodle fettuccine and as spinach fettuccine—fettuccine verde), rigatoni (which is round and hollow, but not long), lumache (which are snail-shaped), farfalle (which are pasta bows), tortellini (which are round and stuffed with chicken), agnolotti (which are pasta squares which you stuff and fold in half, so they are triangle-shaped), cannelloni (which are flat and wide, which you stuff, so they become pasta tubes), lasagna (which are flat and wide, which you layer) and gnocchi (which are dumplings; and which are not made from flour and eggs, like all other pasta, but flour and potatoes). See illustration, p. 35.

Pasta is simple and inexpensive — it appeals to all— and you can put almost anything with it—preferably, fresh vegetables; or seafood or meat. You can prepare something quite special with pasta without being an accomplished chef. And you can mix and match pastas and sauces. For instance, in this book, there is Spaghetti Caponata, but you could also make Fettuccine Caponata. There is Spaghetti Bolognese and there is Tortellini Bolognese; there is Fettuccine con Prosciutto e Piselli and Lumache con Tacchino e Piselli. What is given here is a basic list of recipes for several different kinds of pasta. There are many more kinds of pasta; and the things you can do with pasta could go on forever.

Pasta is a healthy food. When you eat, you take in carbohydrates, protein and fat. In a balanced diet, 60% of what you take in is carbohydrates. What better way to get your carbohydrates than to eat pasta! And pasta has 12% protein (not including what you put on it) and it is low in fat (1.4%). It has vitamins (thiamin—B1; riboflavin—B2; and Niacin) and iron. It's good for you—and it's easy to digest.

Pasta is not fattening—overeating is! In a 4 oz./125 g. serving of pasta, there are approximately 400 calories. Add butter and Parmesan cheese and you have another 100 calories; or add tomato sauce and Parmesan cheese and you have another 125 calories. That's only 500-525 calories! So have a little pasta and relax! Ounce for ounce, pasta has less calories and cholesterol than a steak! Serve with a salad afterwards.

Illustration #4: Pasta. *From left to right:* Farfalle Salmonate, Fettuccine Primavera, Linguine al Pesto. Plates courtesy of Holt Renfrew; serviette and serviette ring courtesy of Georg Jensen.

HOW TO COOK PASTA

1 lb./450 g. pasta	*Add oil and salt to water in a 5 quart/5 L.*
1 tbsp./15 mL. oil	*pot (the oil prevents the pasta sticking).*
1 1/2 tbsp./20 g. salt	*Bring water to a boil on high heat and*
4 quarts/4 L. cold water	*add pasta.*
	Cook al dente—time varies according to
	type of pasta.
	Drain and rinse with cold running water.
	Set aside.

When Cooking Pasta, Follow These Simple Rules:

1.) Never leave the kitchen—pasta takes so little time to cook, you shouldn't have to.
2.) Add oil and salt to water in pot 2 minutes before you add the pasta—to allow the salt to dissolve.
3.) The water must be *rapidly* boiling before you add the pasta.
4.) Stir the pasta in the pot with a wooden spoon.
5.) Cook pasta *al dente*, which means "firm to the bite." Do *not* overcook pasta.
6.) Rinse and toss pasta in a colander as soon as it's cooked *al dente*. Use cold water and do not overrinse. Do not overdrain. Pasta should still be dripping with a little water when you add your sauce.
7.) In most recipes, *add the pasta to the sauce*—not the other way around.
8.) Toss and heat—to warm the pasta—and serve.

PASTA ALL' UVO
Homemade Egg Noodle Pasta

2 1/4 cups/475 g. all-purpose flour
3 eggs
1/2 tsp./2 g. salt

Part One: Making the Dough

Place flour in a mound on a clean flat work surface.
Make a well in the centre of the mound and break eggs into the well.
Add salt to eggs and using a fork or small wire whisk, beat eggs until eggs and salt are mixed together.
Gradually incorporate flour from all sides of the mound into the egg mixture until a thick paste forms.
Once the paste forms, mix in the rest of the flour using your hands.
Work quickly until the dough forms a ball.
If the dough is sticky and moist, add a bit more flour until the dough stops sticking to your hands.
Place dough under a ceramic bowl for 30 minutes.
Clean work area thoroughly, leaving no crumbs of dough on the work surface.
Wash your hands, removing every trace of dough.
Dry hands well.

Part Two: Kneading and Rolling the Dough

Method One: Kneading and Rolling the Dough by Hand

Lightly flour your hands and the work surface.
Begin kneading the dough by slightly flattening the ball of dough and folding it in half towards you.
Knead the dough away from you with the heel of your hand, then fold it over towards you.
Repeat this process, turning the dough around in a circle as you knead it for about 10 minutes until it is smooth and elastic.
(If you are doubling the recipe or using more than 2 eggs, divide the dough in half at this point and put one half of the dough under the ceramic bowl while you work on the other half of the dough.)
Lightly flour the work surface once again and lightly flour a rolling pin.
Slightly flatten the ball of dough once again and begin to roll away from you to open the ball out.
After each roll, rotate the dough so that it stays circular.
Repeat this process until the dough is about 1/8 inch/.25 cm. thick.
In order to get the pasta paper thin, a different method of rolling must be used from now on.
Lightly flour the work surface and the rolling pin once again.
Curl the far end of the dough around the rolling pin and roll towards you, stopping about one-quarter of the way into the dough.
Slide your hands along the dough under the rolling pin, gently stretching it to either side, away from the centre, at the same time as you roll the dough backwards and forwards.

Repeat this process, rolling up a little more dough each time until the entire sheet of dough has been rolled up and stretched.

When the entire sheet of dough has been rolled up on the rolling pin, lift the dough and turn about 45° before unrolling it.

This way, you will start stretching and rolling a new area of the sheet of dough.

Repeat stretching and rolling until pasta sheet is paper thin.

Do not roll dough longer than 10 minutes as it will dry out.

For agnolotti, the dough must be cut, stuffed and boiled right away—it cannot be left to dry (the pasta must be moist so that it will adhere and keep the stuffing in).

For lasagna and fettuccine, lay a clean dry towel on a work surface and lay the dough on the towel, allowing one-third of it to hang over the edge of the table.

Let the dough dry for 30 minutes, turning it over 2 or 3 times.

The pasta is ready to cut when it is dry to the touch.

Do not let it dry too much as it will be impossible to handle.

To cut, place dough on a cutting board.

For lasagna noodles, cut dough into 5 x 3 inch/12.5 x 8 cm. pieces (for easier handling).

Let noodles dry an extra 10 minutes.

For fettuccine, fold dough in a flat roll 3 inches/8 cm. wide and cut across the folded dough.

Cut pasta into desired width of noodles and gently unroll.

Let noodles dry an extra 10 minutes.

Once completely dried, homemade pasta can be stored in a large glass jar, but you will probably want to eat it fresh.

If you are not using it right away, stuffed pasta must be refrigerated or frozen.

Only flat noodles can be rolled and cut by hand.

Method Two: Kneading Dough by Hand and Rolling It through a Pasta Machine

Lightly flour your hands and the work surface.

Begin kneading the dough by slightly flattening the ball of dough and folding it in half towards you.

Knead the dough away from you with the heel of your hand, then fold it over towards you.

Repeat this process, turning the dough around in a circle as you knead it for 3-4 minutes.

Divide the dough into balls the size of oranges.

Work on one ball of dough at a time, leaving the others under a ceramic bowl.

Put pasta machine rollers at the widest setting.

Slightly flatten ball of dough and flour it lightly.

Pass dough through the rollers at the widest setting 5 or 6 times, letting it fold onto itself as it comes through the rollers.

Do not let it fold onto itself the last time it comes through the rollers.

If the dough sticks, dust it with flour.

Adjust the rollers to the next thinnest setting and pass the dough through the rollers once.

Do not let it fold onto itself as it comes through the rollers.

Repeat, adjusting the rollers to the next thinnest setting and so on.

Do not let it fold onto itself as it comes through the rollers.

If the dough sticks, dust it with flour.

If the dough gets too long to handle, cut it in half and process half at a time.

Once the dough has been through the rollers at all settings, lay it between 2 clean cloths.

Repeat for each ball of dough.

If you are making stuffed pasta, proceed with cutting, stuffing and cooking the pasta right away.
The stuffing should be ready at this time.
For lasagna noodles, cut dough into 5 x 3 inch/12.5 x 8 cm. pieces (for easier handling). Let noodles dry an extra 10 minutes.
For fettuccine or other pasta (depending upon your blades), pass the dough through the appropriate cutting blades.
Let noodles dry an extra 10 minutes.

This recipe for Pasta all' Uvo will make enough pasta for 4-6 people. Please note: if pasta is freshly made, it can take as little time as 30 seconds or 1 minute to cook. If pasta is stored for a day or two or bought fresh (which has dried for a day or two), it takes 3-5 minutes to cook.

PASTA VERDE
Homemade Spinach Pasta

8 oz./250 g. fresh spinach
3-3 1/2 cups/700-800 g. all-purpose flour
3 eggs
1/2 tsp./2 g. salt

Wash and stem spinach.
Discard any limp or discoloured leaves.
Steam spinach in boiling water in a covered saucepan for approximately 10 minutes, then drain and cool.
Remove all water from spinach by squeezing spinach by hand, then dry with a clean cloth.
Finely chop spinach, then follow instructions for Pasta all' Uvo, mixing the chopped spinach with the beaten eggs in the well.
When rolling spinach pasta, the dough might require more dusting with flour than egg noodle pasta.

This recipe for Pasta Verde will make enough pasta for 4-6 people. Please note: spinach pasta will take slightly longer to cook than egg noodle pasta. If pasta is freshly made, it can take as little time as 30 seconds or 1 minute to cook. If pasta is stored for a day or two or bought fresh (which has dried out for a day or two), it takes 3-5 minutes to cook.

SPAGHETTINI CON SALMONE AFFUMICATO
Spaghettini with Smoked Salmon

1 lb./450 g. spaghettini	Cook al dente: 3-5 minutes for fresh pasta; 5-7 minutes for packaged spaghettini (see p. 38).

Sauce:

2 cups/450 mL. whipping cream	Cook cream in a large skillet on medium heat until it begins to bubble.
1/4 cup/50 g. butter	Add butter to cream and stir until well blended.
salt (to taste) freshly ground black pepper (to taste)	Season with salt and pepper.
	Add spaghettini to cream and butter. Toss and heat.
4 oz./125 g. smoked salmon, julienned	Add smoked salmon to spaghettini and gently toss.
2 tbsp./30 g. Parmesan cheese, coarsely grated 2 tsp./10 g. fresh parsley, finely chopped	Put spaghettini into a warm serving bowl or on warm plates. Sprinkle with Parmesan cheese and parsley and serve.

This recipe for Spaghettini con Salmone Affumicato serves 4-6 people.

SPAGHETTINI CON MIDOLLO DI BUE
Spaghettini with Bone Marrow

1 lb./450 g. spaghettini	Cook al dente: 3-5 minutes for fresh pasta; 5-7 minutes for packaged spaghettini (see p. 38).

Sauce:

4-6 lbs./2-3 kg. cracked beef marrow bone (yields 6-8 oz./175-250 g. bone marrow)	Extract marrow from cracked beef marrow bone and put it in freezer for 20-30 minutes (to make slicing easier). We recommend that you have your butcher crack the marrow bone.
2 tbsp./30 g. butter 2 tbsp./30 g. fresh parsley, finely chopped	Melt butter in a large skillet on medium heat and add parsley.
6 tbsp./85 mL. dry Marsala wine 3/4 cup/175 mL. beef consommé (see p. 20)	Add wine and beef consommé to butter and parsley and bring to a boil on high heat, then simmer on low heat for 2-3 minutes.

Remove bone marrow from freezer, slice
thinly, add to butter, parsley, wine and
beef consommé and poach on low heat for
4-5 minutes.

salt (to taste)
freshly ground black pepper (to taste)

Season with salt and pepper.

1/2 cup/125 g. Parmesan cheese,
coarsely grated

Gently fold spaghettini and Parmesan
cheese into butter, parsley, wine,
beef consommé and bone marrow.

1/4 cup/50 g. Parmesan cheese,
coarsely grated
2 tsp./10 g. fresh parsley,
finely chopped
freshly ground black pepper (to taste)

Put spaghettini into a warm serving bowl
or on warm plates.
Sprinkle with Parmesan cheese and parsley
and serve with freshly ground black
pepper.

This recipe for Spaghettini con Midollo di Bue serves 4-6 people.

SPAGHETTI ALLA CONTADINA
Spaghetti with Tomatoes and Peppers

Pre-heat oven to 400° F/200° C.

1 lb./450 g. spaghetti

Cook al dente: 3-5 minutes for fresh pasta;
5-7 minutes for packaged spaghetti
(see p. 38).

Sauce:

1/4 cup/50 mL. olive oil
1 small onion, finely chopped
2 cloves garlic, finely chopped

Sauté onion and garlic in oil in a
large skillet on medium heat until onion
is transparent.

4 large ripe tomatoes

Blanch tomatoes by dropping them into a
saucepan of boiling water until skin splits.
Peel, seed and chop tomatoes.
Add tomatoes to onion and garlic.

3 small red peppers

Put peppers in a shallow casserole dish
and bake in oven at 400° F/200° C
for 15-20 minutes.
Allow peppers to cool, then peel, seed
and chop.
Add peppers to onion, garlic
and tomatoes.

1/4 cup/50 mL. dry white wine

Add wine to onion, garlic, tomatoes
and peppers and reduce by simmering
on medium heat for 1-2 minutes.

(cont'd over)

Cont'd from page 43

3/4 cup/175 mL. tomato sauce (see p. 33)	Add tomato sauce, bayleaves and basil to onion, garlic, tomatoes, peppers and wine and simmer on medium heat for 10-15 minutes.
2 bayleaves	
1/8 tsp./pinch of fresh basil, finely chopped	
salt (to taste)	Season with salt and pepper.
freshly ground black pepper (to taste)	
	Add spaghetti to onion, garlic, tomatoes, peppers, wine, tomato sauce, bayleaves and basil. Toss and heat.
1/4 cup/50 g. Parmesan cheese, coarsely grated	Put spaghetti into a warm serving bowl or on warm plates. Sprinkle with Parmesan cheese and parsley and serve.
2 tsp./10 g. fresh parsley, finely chopped	

This recipe for Spaghetti alla Contadina serves 4-6 people.

SPAGHETTI AMATRICIANA
Spaghetti with Tomatoes, Onion, Bacon and Cheese

1 lb./450 g. spaghetti	Cook al dente: 3-5 minutes for fresh pasta; 5-7 minutes for packaged spaghetti (see p. 38).
Sauce:	
1 tsp./5 mL. olive oil	Sauté onion in oil and butter in a large skillet on medium heat until onion is transparent.
1 tsp./5 g. butter	
1 medium onion, finely chopped	
4 oz./125 g. smoked bacon or prosciutto, finely diced	Add bacon or prosciutto to onion and sauté on medium heat for 2-3 minutes.
3 large ripe tomatoes, finely diced	Add tomatoes to onion and bacon or prosciutto.
2 cloves garlic, finely chopped	Add garlic to onion, bacon or prosciutto and tomatoes.
1 tbsp./15 mL. dry white wine	Add wine to onion, bacon or prosciutto, tomatoes and garlic and simmer on medium heat for 3-4 minutes.
freshly ground black pepper (to taste)	Season with pepper only. The bacon or prosciutto should give you enough salt.
	Add spaghetti to onion, bacon or prosciutto, tomatoes, garlic and wine. Toss and heat.

1/4 cup/50 g. Pecorino Romano cheese, coarsely grated	*Put spaghetti into a warm serving bowl or on warm plates. Sprinkle with Pecorino Romano cheese and serve.*

This recipe for Spaghetti Amatriciana serves 4-6 people.

SPAGHETTI BOLOGNESE
Spaghetti with Meat Sauce

Meat Sauce:

3 cups/700 mL. meat sauce (*see p. 34*)	*Prepare the meat sauce first.*
	Prepare pasta 15 minutes before meat sauce is ready. Time your pasta so that it is done al dente at the same time as your sauce is ready.
1 lb./450 g. spaghetti	*Cook al dente: 3-5 minutes for fresh pasta; 5-7 minutes for packaged spaghetti (see p. 38). Drain, but do not rinse.*
1/4 cup/50 g. Parmesan cheese, coarsely grated	*Put spaghetti into a warm serving bowl or on warm plates. Spoon meat sauce over spaghetti, sprinkle with Parmesan cheese and serve.*

This recipe for Spaghetti Bolognese serves 4-6 people.

SPAGHETTI CAPONATA
Spaghetti with Eggplant, Zucchini, Peppers and Tomatoes

1 lb./450 g. spaghetti	*Cook al dente: 3-5 minutes for fresh pasta; 5-7 minutes for packaged spaghetti (see p. 38).*

Sauce:

1/4 cup/50 mL. olive oil 2 tbsp./30 g. butter 2 large ripe tomatoes, chopped 1 small onion, chopped 1/2 cup/125 g. zucchini, diced 1/2 cup/125 g. eggplant, diced 1 medium red or green pepper, sliced 2 cloves garlic, finely chopped	*Sauté tomatoes, onion, zucchini, eggplant, pepper and garlic in oil and butter in a large skillet on medium heat for 8-10 minutes until vegetables are tender.*

(cont'd over)

Cont'd from page 45

1/2 cup/125 mL. tomato sauce *(see p. 33)*	*Add tomato sauce to tomatoes, onion, zucchini, eggplant, pepper and garlic and simmer on medium heat for another 8-10 minutes.*
salt (to taste) freshly ground black pepper (to taste)	*Season with salt and pepper.*
	Add spaghetti to tomatoes, onion, zucchini, eggplant, pepper, garlic and tomato sauce. *Toss and heat.*
1/4 cup/50 g. Parmesan cheese, coarsely grated	*Put spaghetti into a warm serving bowl or on warm plates.* *Sprinkle with Parmesan cheese and serve.*

This recipe for Spaghetti Caponata serves 4-6 people.

SPAGHETTI CARBONARA
Spaghetti with Ham, Eggs and Cream

1 lb./450 g. spaghetti	*Cook al dente: 3-5 minutes for fresh pasta; 5-7 minutes for packaged spaghetti (see p. 38)*
Sauce:	
1 tbsp./15 g. butter 4 oz./125 g. prosciutto, julienned	*Sauté prosciutto in butter in a large skillet on medium heat for 2-3 minutes.*
2 1/2 cups/500 mL. whipping cream	*Add cream to prosciutto and cook on medium heat until cream begins to bubble.*
freshly ground black pepper (to taste)	*Season with pepper only. The prosciutto should give you enough salt.*
	Add spaghetti to prosciutto and cream. *Toss and heat.*
1/2 cup/125 g. Parmesan cheese, coarsely grated	*Gradually add Parmesan cheese to spaghetti.* *Toss together and heat thoroughly until cheese has melted.*
2 egg yolks	*Add egg yolks to spaghetti, toss quickly and remove spaghetti from heat.*

1/2 cup/125 g. Parmesan cheese, coarsely grated	Put spaghetti into a warm serving bowl or on warm plates.
2 tsp./10 g. fresh parsley, finely chopped	Sprinkle with Parmesan cheese and parsley and serve.

This recipe for Spaghetti Carbonara serves 4-6 people.

SPAGHETTI CON CALAMARI
Spaghetti with Squid

1 lb./450 g. spaghetti	Cook al dente: 3-5 minutes for fresh pasta; 5-7 minutes for packaged spaghetti (see p. 38).
Sauce:	
7 oz./200 g. squid	Clean squid (see p. 100) and chop squid (tentacles and body) into 1/2 inch/1 cm. pieces. Pat squid dry with a cloth or paper towel.
1/4 cup/50 mL. olive oil	Sauté squid in hot oil in a skillet on high heat for approximately 15-30 seconds.
1/3 cup/75 mL. dry white wine or dry white vermouth 1 tbsp./15 g. fresh parsley, finely chopped 1 tsp./5 g. hot chili peppers, crushed (approximately 2 pods)	Add wine or vermouth, parsley and chili peppers to squid and simmer on medium heat for 1-2 minutes.
1 cup/250 mL. tomato sauce (see p. 33)	Add tomato sauce to squid, wine or vermouth, parsley and chili peppers, stir until well blended and simmer on medium heat for another 1-2 minutes.
salt (to taste) freshly ground black pepper (to taste)	Season with salt and pepper.
	Add spaghetti to squid, wine or vermouth, parsley, chili peppers and tomato sauce. Toss and heat.
2 tsp./10 g. fresh parsley, finely chopped	Put spaghetti into a warm serving bowl or on warm plates. Sprinkle with parsley and serve.

This recipe for Spaghetti con Calamari serves 4-6 people.

SPAGHETTI CON FEGATINI DI POLLO
Spaghetti with Chicken Livers

1 lb./450 g. spaghetti	Cook al dente: 3-5 minutes for fresh pasta; 5-7 minutes for packaged spaghetti (see p. 38).

Sauce:

2 tbsp./30 g. butter 2 tbsp./30 g. onion, finely chopped 2 cloves garlic, finely chopped	Sauté onion and garlic in butter in a large skillet on medium heat until onion is transparent.
12 oz./350 g. chicken livers	Clean excess tissue and fat from chicken livers and slice thinly. Add chicken livers to onion and garlic and sauté on medium heat for 2-3 minutes.
4 large ripe tomatoes, chopped 1/2 cup/125 mL. dry Marsala wine 1 tsp./5 g. fresh parsley, finely chopped	Add tomatoes, wine and parsley to onion, garlic and chicken livers and simmer on medium heat for approximately 5 minutes.
salt (to taste) freshly ground black pepper (to taste)	Season with salt and pepper.
	Add spaghetti to onion, garlic, chicken livers, tomatoes, wine and parsley. Toss and heat for another 5 minutes.
6 tbsp./85 g. Parmesan cheese, coarsely grated 2 tsp./10 g. fresh parsley, finely chopped	Put spaghetti into a warm serving bowl or on warm plates. Sprinkle with Parmesan cheese and parsley and serve.

This recipe for Spaghetti con Fegatini di Pollo serves 4-6 people.

SPAGHETTI CON TONNO
Spaghetti with Tuna

1 lb./450 g. spaghetti	Cook al dente: 3-5 minutes for fresh pasta; 5-7 minutes for packaged spaghetti (see p. 38).

Sauce:

2 tbsp./30 g. butter 1 small onion, finely chopped 1 clove garlic, finely chopped	Sauté onion and garlic in butter in a large skillet on medium heat until onion is transparent.
2 large tomatoes, chopped 1/4 cup/50 mL. dry red wine 1 (6.5 oz./184 g.) tin of flaked tuna, drained	Add tomatoes, wine and tuna to onion and garlic and simmer on medium heat for 5 minutes.

1 cup/250 mL. tomato sauce (see p. 33)	Add tomato sauce to onion, garlic, tomatoes, wine and tuna and simmer on medium heat for another 1-2 minutes.
	Add spaghetti to onion, garlic, tomatoes, wine, tuna and tomato sauce. Toss and heat.
2 tsp./10 g. fresh parsley, finely chopped	Put spaghetti into a warm serving bowl or on warm plates. Sprinkle with parsley and serve.

This recipe for Spaghetti con Tonno serves 4-6 people.

SPAGHETTI FRUTTI DI MARE
Spaghetti with Seafood

1 lb./450 g. spaghetti	Cook al dente: 3-5 minutes for fresh pasta; 5-7 minutes for packaged spaghetti (see p. 38).
Sauce:	
1 lb./450 g. black mussels	Wash mussels with cold running water to remove sand, then put them in a pot.
1 cup/250 mL. cold water 2 tbsp./30 mL. dry white wine juice of 1/2 lemon	Add water, wine and lemon juice to pot, then cover pot, bring to a boil on high heat and steam mussels for 2-3 minutes until their shells open. Drain pot, reserving 1/2 cup/125 mL. of liquid. Remove mussels from shells (leaving 6 in their shells for garnish).
8 oz./250 g. squid	Clean squid (see p. 100) and chop squid (tentacles and body) into 1/2 inch/1 cm. pieces. Pat squid dry with a cloth or paper towel.
1/3 cup/75 mL. olive oil 1 small onion, chopped	Sauté squid and onion in oil in a large skillet on medium heat until onion is transparent.
4 large ripe tomatoes, chopped 6 large mushrooms, sliced	Add tomatoes and mushrooms to squid, onion and tomatoes and sauté on medium heat for 3 minutes.
1/2 cup/125 mL. dry white wine	Add wine to squid, onion, tomatoes and mushrooms and reduce by simmering on medium heat for 3 minutes.

(cont'd over)

Cont'd from page 49

6 fresh prawns, peeled and cleaned	Add prawns to squid, onion, tomatoes, mushrooms and wine and sauté on medium heat for 3 minutes.
	When prawns are tender, add mussels and simmer on medium heat just long enough to warm them.
salt (to taste) freshly ground black pepper (to taste)	Season with salt and pepper.
	Add spaghetti to squid, onion, tomatoes, mushrooms, wine, prawns and mussels. Toss and heat. If spaghetti is a little dry, add some of the mussel liquid.
6 black mussels 2 tsp./10 g. fresh parsley, finely chopped	Put spaghetti into a warm serving bowl or on warm plates. Garnish with mussels, sprinkle with parsley and serve.

This recipe for Spaghetti Frutti di Mare serves 4-6 people. Spaghetti Frutti di Mare is illustrated on p. 69.

SPAGHETTI MARINARA
Spaghetti with Clams and Tomatoes

1 lb./450 g. spaghetti	Cook al dente: 3-5 minutes for fresh pasta; 5-7 minutes for packaged spaghetti (see p. 38).

Sauce:

6 lbs./3 kg. fresh clams (or 12 oz./ 350 mL. canned clams and clam liquid)	For fresh clams, wash clams with cold running water to remove sand, then put them in a pot.
2 cups/450 mL. cold water 1/4 cup/50 mL. dry white wine 1 small onion, diced 1 bayleaf	Add water, wine, onion and bayleaf to pot, then cover pot, bring to a boil on high heat and steam clams for 7-10 minutes until their shells open. Some clams will not open; discard these. Drain pot, reserving 1/2 cup/125 mL. of liquid. Remove clams from shells.
1/4 cup/50 g. butter 2 shallots, finely chopped 2 cloves garlic, finely chopped	Sauté shallots and garlic in butter in a large skillet on medium heat until shallots are transparent.

3/4 cup/175 mL. dry white wine or dry white vermouth	Add wine or vermouth to shallots and garlic and reduce by simmering on medium heat for 1-2 minutes.
2 tbsp./30 g. fresh parsley, finely chopped	Add clams, clam liquid and parsley to shallots, garlic and wine or vermouth, stir until well blended, then reduce by simmering on medium heat for 2-3 minutes.
4 large ripe tomatoes	Blanch tomatoes by dropping them into a saucepan of boiling water until skin splits. Peel, seed and chop tomatoes. Add tomatoes to shallots, garlic, wine or vermouth, clams, clam liquid and parsley.
3/4 cup/175 mL. tomato sauce (see p. 33)	Add tomato sauce to shallots, garlic, wine or vermouth, clams, clam liquid, parsley and tomatoes and simmer on medium heat for 10 minutes.
salt (to taste) freshly ground black pepper (to taste)	Season with salt and pepper.
	Add spaghetti to shallots, garlic, wine or vermouth, clams, clam liquid, parsley, tomatoes and tomato sauce. Toss and heat.
2 tsp./10 g. fresh parsley, finely chopped	Put spaghetti into a warm serving bowl or on warm plates. Sprinkle with parsley and serve.

This recipe for Spaghetti Marinara serves 4-6 people.

LINGUINE AL PESTO
Linguine with Pesto

1 lb./450 g. linguine	Cook al dente: 3-5 minutes for fresh pasta; 5-7 minutes for packaged linguine (see p. 38).
Pesto Sauce:	
1 cup/250 g. fresh basil 4 sprigs of fresh parsley 2 sprigs of fresh marjoram 4 oz./125 g. pine nuts 2 cloves garlic /3 cup/75 g. Parmesan cheese, coarsely grated 1/3 cup/75 g. Romano cheese, coarsely grated 1/4 cup/50 mL. olive oil 2 tbsp./30 g. butter 1/2 tsp./2 g. salt	Finely chop all ingredients in a blender or food processor, then put in a large skillet.

(cont'd over)

Cont'd from page 51

1/2 cup/125 mL. chicken consommé (see p. 19)	Add chicken consommé to pesto sauce in skillet, stir until well blended and simmer on medium heat for approximately 5 minutes.
	Add linguine to pesto sauce and chicken consommé. Toss and heat.
1/2 cup/125 g. Parmesan cheese, coarsely grated	Put linguine into a warm serving bowl or on warm plates. Sprinkle with Parmesan cheese and serve.

This recipe for Linguine al Pesto serves 4-6 people. The pesto sauce can be made ahead and refrigerated in a sealed glass container for up to 2 weeks. Linguine al Pesto is illustrated on p. 36.

LINGUINE ALLE VONGOLE
Linguine with Clam Sauce

1 lb./450 g. linguine	Cook al dente: 3-5 minutes for fresh pasta; 5-7 minutes for packaged linguine (see p. 38).

Clam Sauce:

6 lbs./3 kg. fresh clams (or 12 oz./ 350 mL. canned clams and clam liquid)	For fresh clams, wash clams with cold running water to remove sand, then put them in a pot.
2 cups/450 mL. cold water 1/4 cup/50 mL. dry white wine 1 small onion, diced 1 bayleaf	Add water, wine, onion and bayleaf to pot, then cover pot, bring to a boil on high heat and steam clams for 7-10 minutes until their shells open. Some clams will not open; discard these. Drain pot, reserving 1/2 cup/125 mL. of liquid. Remove clams from shells.
6 tbsp./85 g. butter 1 1/2 tsp./7 g. garlic, finely chopped	Sauté garlic in butter in a large skillet on medium heat, careful not to burn the garlic.
3 tbsp./45 g. fresh parsley, finely chopped	Add clams, clam liquid and parsley to garlic, stir until well blended and reduce by simmering on medium heat for 4 minutes.
1/3 cup/75 mL. dry white wine	Add wine to garlic, clams, clam liquid and parsley and reduce by simmering on medium heat for 2 minutes.
salt (to taste) freshly ground black pepper (to taste)	Season with salt and pepper.

Add linguine to garlic, clams, clam liquid,
parsley and wine.
Toss and heat.

Put linguine into a warm serving bowl
or on warm plates and serve.

This recipe for Linguine alle Vongole serves 4-6 people.

LINGUINE CON COZZE
Linguine with Mussels

1 lb./450 g. linguine	*Cook al dente: 3-5 minutes for fresh pasta; 5-7 minutes for packaged linguine (see p. 38).*
Sauce:	
4 1/2 lbs./2.25 kg. black mussels	*Wash mussels with cold running water to remove sand, then put them in a pot.*
3 cups/700 mL. cold water 6 tbsp./85 mL. dry white wine	*Add water and wine to pot, then cover pot, bring to a boil on high heat and steam mussels for 2-3 minutes until their shells open.* *Drain pot, reserving half the liquid. Remove mussels from shells (leaving 6 in their shells for garnish).*
2 tbsp./30 g. butter 2 shallots, finely chopped 3 cloves garlic, finely chopped	*Sauté shallots and garlic in butter in a large skillet on medium heat until shallots are transparent.* *Add mussels to shallots and garlic and sauté on medium heat for 2-3 minutes.*
3/4 cup/175 mL. tomato sauce (see p. 33) 1 tbsp./15 g. fresh parsley, finely chopped	*Add tomato sauce, parsley and mussel liquid to shallots, garlic and mussels, stir until well blended, then reduce by simmering on medium heat for 2-3 minutes.*
salt (to taste) freshly ground black pepper (to taste)	*Season with salt and pepper.*
	Add linguine to shallots, garlic, mussels, tomato sauce, parsley and mussel liquid. Toss and heat.
6 black mussels	*Put linguine into a warm serving bowl or on warm plates.* *Garnish with mussels and serve.*

This recipe for Linguine con Cozze serves 4-6 people. Linguine con Cozze is illustrated
on the cover.

LINGUINE GORGONZOLA
Linguine with Gorgonzola Cheese

1 lb./450 g. linguine	Cook al dente: 3-5 minutes for fresh pasta; 5-7 minutes for packaged linguine (see p. 38).
Sauce:	
1 1/2 cups/350 mL. whipping cream	Cook cream in a large skillet on medium heat until it begins to bubble.
6 oz./175 g. Gorgonzola cheese	Crumble Gorgonzola cheese into cream and heat until cheese has melted.
salt (to taste) freshly ground black pepper (to taste)	Season with salt and pepper.
	Add linguine to cream, Gorgonzola cheese and butter. Toss and heat.
1/2 cup/125 g. Parmesan cheese, coarsely grated 4 tbsp./60 g. fresh parsley, finely chopped	Put linguine into a warm serving bowl or on warm plates. Sprinkle with Parmesan cheese and parsley and serve.

This recipe for Linguine Gorgonzola serves 4-6 people.

FETTUCCINE AL BURRO
Fettuccine with Butter

1 lb./450 g. fettuccine	Cook al dente: 3-5 minutes for fresh pasta; 5-7 minutes for packaged fettuccine (see p. 38). Drain, but do not rinse.
	Put fettuccine into a serving bowl.
1/2 cup/125 g. butter	Add butter to fettuccine and toss until butter has melted.
1/2 cup/125 g. Parmesan cheese, coarsely grated	Add Parmesan cheese to fettuccine and butter and toss together.
2 tsp./10 g. fresh parsley, finely chopped freshly ground black pepper (to taste)	Serve fettuccine from the serving bowl or put on warm plates. Sprinkle with parsley and serve with freshly ground black pepper.

This recipe for Fettuccine al Burro serves 4-6 people.

FETTUCCINE ALLA CREMA
Fettuccine with Cream

1 lb./450 g. fettuccine	*Cook al dente: 3-5 minutes for fresh pasta; 5-7 minutes for packaged fettuccine (see p. 38).*
Sauce:	
2 tbsp./30 g. butter	*Melt butter in a large skillet on medium heat.*
2 cups/450 mL. whipping cream	*Add cream to butter and cook on medium heat until cream begins to bubble.*
salt (to taste) freshly ground black pepper (to taste)	*Season with salt and pepper.*
	Add fettuccine to cream. Toss and heat.
2 cups/450 g. Parmesan cheese, coarsely grated	*Gradually add Parmesan cheese to fettuccine. Toss together and heat thoroughly until cheese melts and sauce thickens.*
2 tsp./10 g. fresh parsley, finely chopped	*Put fettuccine into a warm serving bowl or on warm plates. Sprinkle with parsley and serve.*

This recipe for Fettuccine alla Crema serves 4-6 people.

FETTUCCINE ALLA NOCE
Fettuccine with Walnuts

1 lb./450 g. fettuccine	*Cook al dente: 3-5 minutes for fresh pasta; 5-7 minutes for packaged fettuccine (see p. 38).*
Sauce:	
1/4 cup/50 g. butter	*Melt butter in a large skillet on medium heat.*
2 cups/450 mL. whipping cream	*Add cream to butter and cook on medium heat until cream begins to bubble.*
8-9 oz./200-250 g. walnuts, shelled and finely chopped	*Add walnuts (reserving 3 for garnish) to butter and cream and simmer on medium heat for 4-5 minutes, allowing the flavour of the walnuts to mix with the cream.*
salt (to taste) freshly ground black pepper (to taste)	*Season with salt and pepper.*

(cont'd over)

Cont'd from page 55

	Add fettuccine to butter, cream and walnuts. Toss and heat.
3/4 cup/175 g. Parmesan cheese, coarsely grated	Gradually add Parmesan cheese to fettuccine. Toss together and heat thoroughly until cheese melts and sauce thickens.
3 walnuts, halved 2 tsp./10 g. fresh parsley, finely chopped	Put fettuccine into a warm serving bowl or on warm plates. Garnish with walnuts, sprinkle with parsley and serve.

FETTUCCINE CON ANIMELLE
Fettuccine with Sweetbreads

1 lb./450 g. fettuccine	Cook al dente: 3-5 minutes for fresh pasta; 5-7 minutes for packaged fettuccine (see p. 38).
Sauce:	
8 oz./250 g. calf sweetbreads cold water 1 tsp./5 g. salt	Cover sweetbreads with cold water in a saucepan and add salt. Soak sweetbreads for 3-4 hours, changing the water at least once, then drain.
a dash of vinegar or juice of 1/2 lemon	Add vinegar or lemon juice to water in saucepan and bring to a boil on high heat. Add sweetbreads and cook just below the boiling point for approximately 3 minutes until they turn white. Drain and rinse with cold running water. Peel membrane and remove any gristle from sweetbreads, then slice thinly.
1 tbsp./15 g. butter	Sauté sweetbreads in butter in a large skillet on medium heat for 4-5 minutes until they turn golden brown. Remove sweetbreads from skillet and keep warm.
1 cup/250 mL. whipping cream	Add cream to sweetbread juices in skillet, stir until well blended and cook on medium heat until cream begins to bubble. Add sweetbreads to cream.
salt (to taste) freshly ground black pepper (to taste)	Season with salt and pepper.

	Add fettuccine to sweetbreads and cream. Toss and heat.
2 tbsp./30 g. butter 2 cups/450 g. Parmesan cheese, coarsely grated	Gradually add butter and Parmesan cheese to fettuccine. Toss together and heat thoroughly until butter and cheese have melted.
1/2 cup/125 g. Parmesan cheese, coarsely grated 2 tsp./10 g. fresh parsley, finely chopped	Put fettuccine into a warm serving bowl or on warm plates. Sprinkle with Parmesan cheese and parsley and serve.

FETTUCCINE CON ASPARAGI
Fettuccine with Asparagus

1 lb./450 g. fettuccine	Cook al dente: 3-5 minutes for fresh pasta; 5-7 minutes for packaged fettuccine (see p. 38).
Sauce:	
2 lbs./1 kg. fresh asparagus salt (to taste)	Tie asparagus together in a bundle and blanch by dropping into a saucepan of boiling salted water for approximately 2 minutes. Drain and rinse with cold running water. Set aside. When asparagus is cool, cut off the tips.
1/4 cup/50 g. butter	Gently sauté asparagus tips in butter in a large skillet on medium heat for 1-2 minutes.
1 cup/250 mL. whipping cream	Add cream to asparagus tips and cook on medium heat until cream begins to bubble.
salt (to taste) freshly ground black pepper (to taste)	Season with salt and pepper.
	Add fettuccine to asparagus tips and cream. Toss gently, careful not to mash the asparagus tips, and heat.
1/2 cup/125 g. Parmesan cheese, coarsely grated	Gradually add Parmesan cheese to fettuccine. Toss together and heat thoroughly until cheese has melted.
2 tbsp./30 g. fresh parsley, finely chopped	Put fettuccine into a warm serving bowl or on warm plates. Sprinkle with parsley and serve.

This recipe for Fettuccine con Asparagi serves 4-6 people. The recipe for Fettuccine alla Noce on pp. 55-56 and the recipe for Fettuccine con Animelle (above) also serve 4-6 people.

FETTUCCINE CON CARCIOFI
Fettuccine with Artichokes

1 lb./450 g. fettuccine	Cook al dente: 3-5 minutes for fresh pasta; 5-7 minutes for packaged fettuccine (see p. 38).

Sauce:

1/4 cup/50 g. butter 2 cloves garlic, finely chopped	Sauté garlic in butter in a large skillet on medium heat, careful not to burn the garlic.
1 (14 oz./398 mL.) can of artichoke hearts, drained and quartered 1/4 cup/50 mL. dry white wine	Add wine to garlic and artichoke hearts and simmer on medium heat for 1-2 minutes.
2 1/2 cups/500 mL. whipping cream	Add cream to garlic, artichoke hearts and wine, stir until well blended and cook on medium heat until cream begins to bubble.
salt (to taste) freshly ground black pepper (to taste)	Season with salt and pepper.
	Add fettuccine to garlic, artichoke hearts, wine and cream. Toss and heat.
1/2 cup/125 g. Parmesan cheese, coarsely grated	Gradually add Parmesan cheese to fettuccine. Toss together and heat thoroughly until cheese has melted.
2 tsp./10 g. fresh parsley, finely chopped	Put fettuccine into a warm serving bowl or on warm plates. Sprinkle with parsley and serve.

This recipe for Fettuccine con Carciofi serves 4-6 people.

FETTUCCINE CON CAVIALE
Fettuccine with Caviar

1 lb./450 g. fettuccine	Cook al dente: 3-5 minutes for fresh pasta; 5-7 minutes for packaged fettuccine (see p. 38).

Sauce:

2 tbsp./30 g. butter	Melt butter in a large skillet on medium heat.
2 cups/450 mL. whipping cream	Add cream to butter and cook on medium heat until cream begins to bubble.

	Add fettuccine to cream. *Toss and heat.*
2 cups/450 g. Parmesan cheese, coarsely grated	*Gradually add Parmesan cheese to fettuccine.* *Toss together and heat thoroughly until cheese has melted.*
freshly ground black pepper (to taste)	*Season with pepper only.*
1 (3 1/2 oz./100 g.) jar of lumpfish or salmon caviar	*Gently fold caviar into fettuccine just before serving.*
2 tsp./10 g. fresh parsley, finely chopped	*Put fettuccine into a warm serving bowl or on warm plates.* *Sprinkle with parsley and serve.*

This recipe for Fettuccine con Caviale serves 4-6 people.

FETTUCCINE CON GAMBERETTI
Fettuccine with Shrimp

1 lb./450 g. fettuccine	*Cook al dente: 3-5 minutes for fresh pasta; 5-7 minutes for packaged fettuccine (see p. 38).*
Sauce:	
1 tbsp./15 g. butter 8 oz./250 g. fresh baby shrimp	*Gently sauté shrimp in butter in a large skillet on medium heat for 1-2 minutes.*
1/4 cup/50 mL. dry white wine	*Add wine to shrimp and simmer on medium heat for 1-2 minutes.*
1 cup/250 mL. whipping cream	*Add cream to shrimp and wine and cook on medium heat until cream begins to bubble.*
salt (to taste) freshly ground black pepper (to taste)	*Season with salt and pepper.*
	Add fettuccine to shrimp, wine and cream. *Toss and heat.*
1/2 cup/125 g. Parmesan cheese, coarsely grated	*Gradually add Parmesan cheese to fettuccine.* *Toss together and heat thoroughly until cheese has melted.*
4 tsp./20 g. Parmesan cheese, coarsely grated 2 tsp./10 g. fresh parsley, finely chopped	*Put fettuccine into a warm serving bowl or on warm plates.* *Sprinkle with Parmesan cheese and parsley and serve.*

This recipe for Fettuccine con Gamberetti serves 4-6 people.

FETTUCCINE CON MELANZANE
Fettuccine with Eggplant

1 lb./450 g. fettuccine	*Cook al dente: 3-5 minutes for fresh pasta; 5-7 minutes for packaged fettuccine (see p. 38).*

Sauce:

1 tbsp./15 mL. olive oil 2 tbsp./30 g. butter 1 small onion, diced	*Sauté onion in oil and butter in a large skillet on medium heat until onion is transparent.*
3 large ripe tomatoes	*Blanch tomatoes by dropping them into a saucepan of boiling water until skin splits. Peel, seed and chop tomatoes. Add tomatoes to onion.*
1 small eggplant, finely diced 2 cloves garlic, finely chopped	*Add eggplant and garlic to onion and tomatoes and sauté on medium heat for approximately 5 minutes.*
1/4 cup/50 mL. chicken consommé (see p. 19) 1 tsp./5 g. fresh parsley, finely chopped 1/2 tsp./2 g. fresh oregano	*Add chicken consommé, parsley and oregano to onion, tomatoes, eggplant and garlic and simmer on medium heat for 1-2 minutes.*
salt (to taste) freshly ground black pepper (to taste)	*Season with salt and pepper.*
	Add fettuccine to onion, tomatoes, eggplant, garlic, chicken consommé, parsley and oregano. Toss and heat.
1/2 cup/125 g. Parmesan cheese, coarsely grated	*Gradually add Parmesan cheese to fettuccine. Toss together and heat thoroughly until cheese has melted.*
1/2 cup/125 g. Parmesan cheese, coarsely grated 2 tsp./10 g. fresh parsley, finely chopped	*Put fettuccine into a warm serving bowl or on warm plates. Sprinkle with Parmesan cheese and parsley and serve.*

This recipe for Fettuccine con Melanzane serves 4-6 people.

FETTUCCINE CON PORRI
Fettuccine with Leeks

1 lb./450 g. fettuccine

Cook al dente: 3-5 minutes for fresh pasta; 5-7 minutes for packaged fettuccine (see p. 38).

Sauce:

2 large or 3 small leeks

Wash leeks carefully. Remove root and discard one-third from top of leeks, then cut into thin strips 2 inches/5 cm. in length.

2 tbsp./30 g. butter
2 cloves garlic, finely chopped

Sauté leeks and garlic in butter in a large skillet on medium heat for 7-10 minutes until leeks are soft.

1/2 cup/125 mL. dry white wine

Add wine to leeks and garlic and reduce by simmering on medium heat for 1-2 minutes.

1 cup/250 mL. chicken consommé (see p. 19)

Add chicken consommé to leeks, garlic and wine and reduce by simmering on medium heat for 2-3 minutes.

1 cup/250 mL. whipping cream

Add cream to leeks, garlic, wine and chicken consommé and cook on medium heat until cream begins to bubble.

salt (to taste)
freshly ground black pepper (to taste)

Season with salt and pepper.

Add fettuccine to leeks, garlic, wine, chicken consommé and cream. Toss and heat.

1/2 cup/125 g. Parmesan cheese, coarsely grated

Gradually add Parmesan cheese to fettuccine. Toss together and heat thoroughly until cheese has melted.

1/4 cup/50 g. Parmesan cheese, coarsely grated
2 tsp./10 g. fresh parsley, finely chopped

Put fettuccine into a warm serving bowl or on warm plates. Sprinkle with Parmesan cheese and parsley and serve.

This recipe for Fettuccine con Porri serves 4-6 people.

FETTUCCINE CON PROSCIUTTO E PISELLI
Fettuccine with Prosciutto and Peas

1 lb./450 g. fettuccine	Cook al dente: 3-5 minutes for fresh pasta; 5-7 minutes for packaged fettuccine (see p. 38).
Sauce:	
2 tbsp./30 g. butter 2 tbsp./30 mL. dry white wine 6 tbsp./85 g. petit pois	Sauté peas in butter and wine in a large skillet on medium heat for 2-3 minutes.
2 cups/450 mL. whipping cream	Add cream to peas and cook on medium heat until cream begins to bubble.
2 oz./50 g. prosciutto, julienned	Add prosciutto to peas and cream and simmer on medium heat for 2-3 minutes.
salt (to taste) freshly ground black pepper (to taste)	Season with salt and pepper, but use less salt than you normally would use. The prosciutto will give you some salt.
	Add fettuccine to peas, cream and prosciutto.
1 cup/250 g. Parmesan cheese, coarsely grated	Gradually add Parmesan cheese to fettuccine. Toss together and heat thoroughly until cheese has melted.
1/2 cup/125 g. Parmesan cheese, coarsely grated 2 tsp./10 g. fresh parsley, finely chopped	Put fettuccine into a warm serving bowl or on warm plates. Sprinkle with Parmesan cheese and parsley and serve.

This recipe for Fettuccine con Prosciutto e Piselli serves 4-6 people.

FETTUCCINE CON QUATTRO FORMAGGI
Fettuccine with Four Cheeses

1 lb./450 g. fettuccine	Cook al dente: 3-5 minutes for fresh pasta; 5-7 minutes for packaged fettuccine (see p. 38).
Sauce:	
1/4 cup/50 g. butter	Melt butter in a large skillet on medium heat.
1 1/2 cups/350 mL. whipping cream	Add cream to butter and cook on medium heat until cream begins to bubble.
freshly ground black pepper (to taste)	Season with pepper only.

	Add fettuccine to cream. Toss and heat.
2 tbsp./30 g. Parmesan cheese, coarsely grated 2 tbsp./30 g. Fontina cheese, grated 2 tbsp./30 g. Gorgonzola cheese, crumbled 2 tbsp./30 g. Provolone cheese, grated	Gradually add Parmesan, Fontina, Gorgonzola and Provolone cheese to fettuccine. Toss together and heat thoroughly until cheese has melted.
1/4 cup/50 g. Parmesan cheese, coarsely grated 2 tsp./10 g. fresh parsley, finely chopped	Put fettuccine into a warm serving bowl or on warm plates. Sprinkle with Parmesan cheese and parsley and serve.

FETTUCCINE CON ZUCCHINI
Fettuccine with Zucchini

1 lb./450 g. fettuccine	Cook al dente: 3-5 minutes for fresh pasta; 5-7 minutes for packaged fettuccine (see p. 38).
Sauce:	
1/4 cup/50 g. butter 1 cup/250 g. zucchini, thinly sliced	Sauté zucchini in butter in a large skillet on medium heat for 1-2 minutes.
2 cloves garlic, finely chopped	Add garlic to zucchini and sauté on medium heat for another 2 minutes.
1/2 cup/125 mL. chicken consommé (see p. 25) 2 tsp./10 g. fresh parsley, finely chopped	Add chicken consommé and parsley to zucchini and simmer on medium heat for 2-3 minutes.
salt (to taste) white pepper (to taste)	Season with salt and pepper.
	Add fettuccine to zucchini, chicken consommé and parsley. Toss and heat.
1/2 cup/125 g. Parmesan cheese, coarsely grated	Gradually add Parmesan cheese to fettuccine. Toss together and heat thoroughly until cheese has melted.
2 tsp./10 g. fresh parsley, finely chopped	Put fettuccine into a warm serving bowl or on warm plates. Sprinkle with parsley and serve.

This recipe for Fettuccine con Zucchini serves 4-6 people. The recipe for Fettuccine con Quattro Formaggi (above) also serves 4-6 people.

FETTUCCINE PRIMAVERA
Fettuccine with Fresh Vegetables

	Pre-heat oven to 400° F/200° C.
1 lb./450 g. fettuccine	*Cook al dente: 3-5 minutes for fresh pasta, 5-7 minutes for packaged fettuccine (see p. 38).*
Sauce:	
2 large ripe tomatoes	*Blanch tomatoes by dropping them into a saucepan of boiling water until skin splits. Peel, seed and julienne tomatoes.*
1 red pepper	*Put pepper in a shallow casserole dish in oven and bake at 400° F/200° C for 15-20 minutes. Allow pepper to cool, then peel, seed and julienne.*
1/4 cup/50 g. butter 1 small carrot, julienned 1 small zucchini, julienned 1/2 cup/125 g. cauliflower flowerets 1/2 cup/125 g. broccoli flowerets 1/3 cup/75 g. snow peas 2 cloves garlic, finely chopped	*Sauté tomatoes, pepper, carrot, zucchini, cauliflower flowerets, broccoli flowerets, snow peas and garlic in butter in a large skillet on medium heat for 5-6 minutes.*
2 cups/450 mL. whipping cream	*Add cream to tomatoes, pepper, carrot, zucchini, cauliflower flowerets, broccoli flowerets, snow peas and garlic and cook on medium heat until cream begins to bubble.*
salt (to taste) freshly ground black pepper (to taste)	*Season with salt and pepper.*
	Add fettuccine to tomatoes, pepper, carrot, zucchini, cauliflower flowerets, broccoli flowerets, snow peas, garlic and cream. Toss and heat.
1/4 cup/50 g. Parmesan cheese, coarsely grated	*Gradually add Parmesan cheese to fettuccine. Toss together and heat thoroughly until cheese has melted.*
1/4 cup/50 g. Parmesan cheese, coarsely grated 2 tsp./10 g. fresh parsley, finely chopped	*Put fettuccine into a warm serving bowl or on warm plates. Sprinkle with Parmesan cheese and parsley and serve.*

This recipe for Fettuccine Primavera serves 4-6 people. Fettuccine Primavera is illustrated on p. 36.

FETTUCCINE SCALOPPATE
Fettuccine with Scallops

1 lb./450 g. fettuccine	*Cook al dente: 3-5 minutes for fresh pasta; 5-7 minutes for packaged fettuccine (see p. 38).*

Sauce:

1/2 cup/125 g. butter 1/4 cup/50 g. onion, finely chopped 4 mushrooms, thinly sliced	*Sauté onion and mushrooms in butter in a large skillet on medium heat until onion is transparent.*
12 oz./350 g. fresh scallops	*Add scallops to onion and mushrooms and sauté on high heat for approximately 5 minutes, stirring constantly.*
1/4 cup/50 mL. dry white wine	*Add wine to onion, mushrooms and scallops and reduce by simmering on medium heat for 1-2 minutes.*
1/2 cup/125 mL. whipping cream 2 tsp./10 mL. lemon juice	*Add cream and lemon juice to onion, mushrooms, scallops and wine, stir until well blended and cook on medium heat until cream begins to bubble.*
1 tbsp./15 g. fresh parsley, finely chopped	*Add parsley to onion, mushrooms, scallops, wine, cream and lemon juice and stir until well blended.*
salt (to taste) freshly ground black pepper (to taste)	*Season with salt and pepper.*
	Add fettuccine to onion, mushrooms, scallops, wine, cream, lemon juice and parsley. Toss and heat.
2 tsp./10 g. fresh parsley, finely chopped	*Put fettuccine into a warm serving bowl or on warm plates. Sprinkle with parsley and serve.*

This recipe for Fettuccine Scaloppate serves 4-6 people.

FETTUCCINE VERDE ALLA CREMA
Spinach Fettuccine in Cream

1 lb./450 g. fettuccine	*Cook al dente: 3-5 minutes for fresh pasta; 5-7 minutes for packaged fettuccine (see p. 38).*

(cont'd over)

Cont'd from page 65

Sauce:

2 tbsp./30 g. butter	Melt butter in a large skillet on medium heat.
2 cups/450 mL. whipping cream	Add cream to butter and cook on medium heat until cream begins to bubble.
salt (to taste) freshly ground black pepper (to taste)	Season with salt and pepper.
	Add fettuccine to cream. Toss and heat.
1 cup/250 g. Parmesan cheese, coarsely grated	Gradually add Parmesan cheese to fettuccine. Toss together and heat thoroughly until cheese has melted.
1/4 cup/50 g. Parmesan cheese, coarsely grated 2 tsp./10 g. fresh parsley, finely chopped	Put fettuccine into a warm serving bowl or on warm plates. Sprinkle with Parmesan cheese and parsley and serve.

This recipe for Fettuccine Verde alla Crema serves 4-6 people.

FETTUCCINE VERDE CON PATATE
Spinach Fettuccine with Potatoes

1 lb./450 g. fettuccine	Cook al dente: 3-5 minutes for fresh pasta; 5-7 minutes for packaged fettuccine (see p. 38).

Sauce:

1/4 cup/50 g. butter 2 medium potatoes, peeled and thinly sliced 2 tbsp./30 g. onion, finely chopped	Sauté potatoes and onion in butter in a large skillet on medium heat for approximately 5 minutes.
3/4 cup/175 mL. chicken consommé (see p. 19) 3/4 cup/175 mL. whipping cream	Add chicken consommé and cream to potatoes and onion, stir until well blended and cook on medium heat until cream begins to bubble and potatoes are cooked.
salt (to taste) freshly ground black pepper (to taste)	Season with salt and pepper.
	Add fettuccine to potatoes, onion, chicken consommé and cream. Toss and heat.

1/2 cup/125 g. Parmesan cheese, coarsely grated	*Gradually add Parmesan cheese to fettuccine.* *Toss together and heat thoroughly until cheese has melted.*
1/4 cup/50 g. Parmesan cheese, coarsely grated 2 tsp./10 g. fresh parsley, finely chopped	*Put fettuccine into a warm serving bowl or on warm plates.* *Sprinkle with Parmesan cheese and parsley and serve.*

This recipe for Fettuccine Verdi con Patate serves 4-6 people.

PASTICCIO DI RIGATONI
Rigatoni Baked with Cream and Cheese

	Pre-heat oven to 375° F/190° C.
1 lb./450 g. rigatoni	*Cook rigatoni for only 5 minutes, then drain and rinse.*
2 tbsp./30 g. butter	*Butter the bottom of a casserole dish and put a bed of rigatoni in the bottom of the dish.*
1/2 cup/125 mL. white sauce (*see p. 32*)	*Pour white sauce over rigatoni.*
1/2 cup/125 mL. whipping cream	*Pour cream over rigatoni and white sauce.*
1/2 cup/125 g. Parmesan cheese, coarsely grated	*Sprinkle Parmesan cheese over rigatoni, white sauce and cream.*
	Put remaining rigatoni on top of white sauce, cream and Parmesan cheese.
1/2 cup/125 mL. white sauce (*see p. 32*)	*Cover second layer of rigatoni with white sauce.*
1/2 cup/125 mL. whipping cream	*Pour cream over second layer of rigatoni and white sauce.*
1/2 cup/125 g. Parmesan cheese	*Sprinkle Parmesan cheese over rigatoni, white sauce and cream.*
freshly ground black pepper (to taste) 1/8 tsp./pinch of paprika (for colour)	*Season with pepper only and sprinkle with paprika.*
	Put casserole dish in oven and bake at 375° F/190° C for 20 minutes.
	Serve rigatoni from casserole dish or put on warm plates and serve.

This recipe for Pasticcio di Rigatoni serves 4-6 people.

RIGATONI AL PEPERONCINO ROSSO
Rigatoni with Red Peppers

Pre-heat oven to 400° F/200° C.

1 lb./450 g. rigatoni	*Cook al dente: 5-7 minutes for fresh pasta; 10-15 minutes for packaged rigatoni (see p. 38).*

Sauce:

4 red peppers — *Put peppers in a shallow casserole dish and bake in oven at 400° F/200° C for 15-20 minutes.*
Allow peppers to cool, then peel, seed and slice.

1/2 cup/125 g. butter
1/4 cup/50 g. onion, finely chopped
2 cloves garlic, finely chopped

Sauté peppers, onion and garlic in butter in a large skillet on medium heat until onion is transparent.

2 large ripe tomatoes — *Blanch tomatoes by dropping them into a saucepan of boiling water until skin splits. Peel, seed and chop tomatoes.*
Add tomatoes to peppers, onion and garlic.

3/4 cup/175 mL. dry white wine
1 tbsp./15 g. fresh parsley, finely chopped
1 small bayleaf, crushed

Add wine, parsley and bayleaf to peppers, onion, garlic and tomatoes and simmer on medium heat for approximately 5 minutes.

salt (to taste)
freshly ground black pepper (to taste)

Season with salt and pepper.

Add rigatoni to peppers, onion, garlic, tomatoes, wine, parsley and bayleaf.
Toss and heat.

1/4 cup/50 g. Parmesan cheese, coarsely grated
2 tsp./10 g. fresh parsley, finely chopped

Put rigatoni into a warm serving bowl or on warm plates.
Sprinkle with Parmesan cheese and parsley and serve.

This recipe for Rigatoni al Peperoncino Rosso serves 4-6 people. Rigatoni al Peperoncino Rosso is illustrated on the page opposite.

Illustration #5: Pasta. *From left to right:* Lumache con Tacchino e Piselli (*upper plate*), Spaghetti Frutti di Mare (*lower plate*) and Rigatoni al Peperoncino Rosso. Tiles courtesy of World Mosaic Ltd.; plates courtesy of Holt Renfrew; serviettes and serviette rings courtesy of Georg Jensen.

RIGATONI CON ACCIUGHE
Rigatoni with Anchovies

Pre-heat oven to 400° F/200° C.

1 lb./450 g. rigatoni	*Cook al dente: 5-7 minutes for fresh pasta; 10-15 minutes for packaged rigatoni (see p. 38).*

Sauce:

1 red or green pepper	*Put pepper in a shallow casserole dish and bake in oven at 400° F/200° C for 15-20 minutes. Allow peppers to cool, then peel, seed and chop.*
1/4 cup/50 mL. olive oil 2 cloves garlic, finely chopped	*Sauté pepper and garlic in oil in a large skillet on medium heat for 2-3 minutes.*
6 medium ripe tomatoes	*Blanch tomatoes by dropping them into a saucepan of boiling water until skin splits. Peel, seed and chop tomatoes. Add tomatoes to pepper and garlic.*
8 anchovy fillets, washed, pounded and chopped 1/4 cup/50 mL. dry white wine	*Add anchovies and wine to pepper, garlic and tomatoes and simmer on medium heat for 10-12 minutes.*
salt (to taste) freshly ground black pepper (to taste)	*Season with salt and pepper, but use less salt than you normally would use. Anchovies are salty.*
	Add rigatoni to pepper, garlic, tomatoes, anchovies and wine. Toss and heat.
2 tsp./10 g. fresh parsley, finely chopped	*Put rigatoni into a warm serving bowl or on warm plates. Sprinkle with parsley and serve.*

This recipe for Rigatoni con Acciughe serves 4-6 people.

RIGATONI CONCHIGLIE DI MARE
Rigatoni with Scallops

1 lb./450 g. rigatoni	*Cook al dente: 5-7 minutes for fresh pasta; 10-15 minutes for packaged rigatoni (see p. 38).*

(cont'd over)

Illustration #6: Pasta. *From left to right:* Lasagna al Forno (*upper plate*), Cannelloni alla Fiorentina (*lower plate*) and Agnolotti con Ricotta e Spinaci. Tiles courtesy of World Mosaic Ltd.; plates and salt and pepper courtesy of Holt Renfrew.

Cont'd from page 71

Sauce:

1/4 cup/50 g. butter 1 tbsp./15 g. onion, finely chopped	*Sauté onion in butter in a large skillet on medium heat until onion is transparent.*
8 oz./250 g. fresh scallops, sliced in half	*Add scallops to onion and sauté on medium heat for 2-3 minutes.*
1/4 cup/50 mL. brandy	*Add brandy to onion and scallops and stir until well blended.*
1 cup/250 mL. whipping cream	*Add cream to onion, scallops and brandy, stir until well blended and cook on medium heat until cream begins to bubble.*
salt (to taste) freshly ground black pepper (to taste)	*Season with salt and pepper.*
	Add rigatoni to onion, scallops, brandy and cream. *Toss and cook rigatoni for another 2 minutes to allow the cream to mix with the rigatoni.*
1/2 cup/125 g. Parmesan cheese, coarsely grated	*Gradually add Parmesan cheese to rigatoni.* *Toss together and heat thoroughly until cheese has melted.*
2 tbsp./30 g. fresh parsley, finely chopped	*Put rigatoni into a warm serving bowl or on warm plates.* *Sprinkle with parsley and serve.*

This recipe for Rigatoni Conchiglie di Mare serves 4-6 people.

RIGATONI DEL CAMINETTO
Rigatoni with Parsley, Garlic Butter, Italian Sausage and Red Peppers

	Pre-heat oven to 400° F/200° C.
1 lb./450 g. rigatoni	*Cook al dente: 5-7 minutes for fresh pasta; 10-15 minutes for packaged rigatoni (see p. 38).*
Sauce:	
4 red peppers	*Put peppers in a shallow casserole dish and bake in oven at 400° F/200° C for 15-20 minutes.* *Allow peppers to cool, then peel, seed and slice.*

1/2 cup/125 g. butter 3 cloves garlic, finely chopped	*Sauté peppers and garlic in butter in a large skillet on medium heat for 2-3 minutes.*
2 oz./50 g. Italian sausage, finely diced 1 1/2 tbsp./20 g. fresh parsley, finely chopped	*Add sausage and parsley to peppers and garlic and simmer, partly covered, on medium heat for 2-3 minutes, stirring occasionally.*
salt (to taste) freshly ground black pepper (to taste)	*Season with salt and pepper.*
	Add rigatoni to peppers, garlic, sausage and parsley. Toss and heat.
1/2 cup/125 g. Parmesan cheese, coarsely grated	*Gradually add Parmesan cheese to rigatoni. Toss together and heat thoroughly until cheese has melted.*
2 tsp./10 g. fresh parsley, finely chopped	*Put rigatoni into a warm serving bowl or on warm plates. Sprinkle with parsley and serve.*

This recipe for Rigatoni del Caminetto serves 4-6 people.

RIGATONI DELL' ORTOLANO
Cold Vegetable and Herb Rigatoni

1 lb./450 g. rigatoni 1 1/2 tbsp./20 g. salt 4 quarts/4 L. cold water 2 tbsp./30 mL. olive oil	*Add salt to water in a 5 quart/5 L. pot. Bring water to boil on high heat and add rigatoni. Cook al dente: 5-7 minutes for fresh pasta; 10-15 minutes for packaged rigatoni. Drain and rinse with cold running water. Add oil to rigatoni after draining and rinsing (the oil prevents the pasta sticking). Set aside.*
1 small carrot, julienned 1/3 cup/75 g. broccoli flowerets 1/3 cup/75 g. snow peas	*Steam carrot, broccoli flowerets and snow peas in a small amount of boiling water for 3-4 minutes. Drain and rinse with cold running water. Set aside.*
1 red or yellow pepper, seeded and julienned	*Put rigatoni, carrot, broccoli flowerets, snow peas and red or yellow pepper together in a bowl.*
salt (to taste) freshly ground black pepper (to taste)	*Season with salt and pepper.*

(cont'd over)

Cont'd from page 73

2 tsp./10g. fresh basil, finely chopped 1 tbsp./15 g. fresh parsley, finely chopped	Add basil and parsley to rigatoni, carrot, broccoli flowerets, snow peas and red or yellow pepper.
1 cup/250 mL. mayonnaise, made with vegetable oil (see p. 163)	Fold mayonnaise into rigatoni, carrot, broccoli flowerets, snow peas, red or yellow pepper, basil and parsley. Refrigerate rigatoni for at least 1 hour.
4-6 leaves of fresh basil or 4-6 sprigs of fresh parsley	Put rigatoni into a serving bowl or on plates. Garnish with basil leaves or sprigs of parsley and serve.

FARFALLE SALMONATE
Pasta Bows with Salmon

1 lb./450 g. farfalle	Cook al dente: 5-7 minutes for packaged farfalle (see p. 38).
Sauce:	
2 tbsp./30 g. butter 1 small onion, finely chopped 2 cloves garlic, finely chopped	Sauté onion and garlic in butter in a large skillet on medium heat until onion is transparent.
1 lb./450 g. fillet of salmon, diced small	Add salmon to onion and garlic and sauté on medium heat for 2-3 minutes.
1/4 cup/50 mL. brandy 1/4 cup/50 mL. dry white wine	Add brandy and wine to onion, garlic and salmon, stir until well blended and reduce by simmering on medium heat for 1-2 minutes.
3 cups/700 mL. tomato sauce (see p. 33)	Add tomato sauce to onion, garlic, salmon, brandy and wine, stir until well blended and simmer on medium heat until warm.
salt (to taste) freshly ground black pepper (to taste)	Season with salt and pepper. Add farfalle to onion, garlic, salmon, brandy, wine and tomato sauce. Toss and heat. Put farfalle into a warm serving bowl or on warm plates and serve.

This recipe for Farfalle Salmonate serves 4-6 people. Farfalle Salmonate is illustrated on p. 36. The recipe for Rigatoni dell' Ortolano (above) serves 4-6 people.

FARFALLE CON ROGNONCINI AL FUNGHETTO
Pasta Bows with Kidneys and Mushrooms

1 lb./450 g. farfalle	*Cook al dente: 5-7 minutes for packaged farfalle (see p. 38).*
Sauce:	
1 cup/250 g. fresh mushrooms	*Wash mushrooms and dry them with a cloth or paper towel, then slice.*
oil	*Coat the bottom of a skillet in oil and sauté mushrooms in oil in skillet on medium heat for 3 minutes.*
2 veal kidneys, cleaned and diced 2 cloves garlic, finely chopped 1 tbsp./15 g. fresh parsley, finely chopped	*Add kidneys, garlic and parsley to mushrooms and sauté on medium heat for 2-3 minutes.*
1/4 cup/50 mL. Madeira wine or dry Marsala wine	*Add wine to mushrooms, kidneys, garlic and parsley and stir until well blended.*
3/4 cup/175 mL. whipping cream	*Add cream to mushrooms, kidneys, garlic, parsley and wine, stir until well blended and cook on medium heat until cream begins to bubble.*
salt (to taste) freshly ground black pepper (to taste)	*Season with salt and pepper.*
	Add farfalle to mushrooms, kidneys, garlic, parsley, wine and cream. *Toss and heat.*
1/4 cup/50 g. Parmesan cheese, coarsely grated 2 tsp./10 g. fresh parsley, finely chopped	*Put farfalle into a warm serving bowl or on warm plates.* *Sprinkle with Parmesan cheese and parsley and serve.*

This recipe for Farfalle con Rognoncini al Funghetto serves 4-6 people.

LUMACHE CON TACCHINO E PISELLI
Lumache with Turkey and Peas

1 lb./450 g. lumache	*Cook al dente: 3-5 minutes for fresh pasta; 5-7 minutes for packaged lumache (see p. 38).*

(cont'd over)

Cont'd from page 75

Sauce:

1/4 cup/50 g. butter 12-14 oz./350-400 g. cooked turkey breast, diced or julienned	Sauté turkey in butter in a large skillet on medium heat for 1-2 minutes.
1/4 cup/50 mL. dry white wine	Add wine to turkey and butter and reduce by simmering on medium heat for 1-2 minutes.
6 tbsp./85 g. petit pois 1/8 tsp./pinch of fresh thyme, torn small	Add peas and thyme to turkey, butter and wine and simmer on medium heat for 1-2 minutes.
2 cups/450 mL. whipping cream	Add cream to turkey, butter, wine and peas and cook on medium heat until cream begins to bubble.
salt (to taste) freshly ground black pepper (to taste)	Season with salt and pepper.
	Add lumache to turkey, butter, wine, peas and cream. Toss and heat.
1 cup/250 g. Parmesan cheese, coarsely grated	Gradually add Parmesan cheese to lumache. Toss together and heat thoroughly until cheese has melted.
4-6 sprigs of fresh thyme 1/4 cup/50 g. Parmesan cheese, coarsely grated	Put lumache into a warm serving bowl or on warm plates. Garnish with sprigs of thyme, sprinkle with Parmesan cheese and serve.

This recipe for Lumache con Tacchino e Piselli serves 4-6 people. Lumache con Tacchino e Piselli is illustrated on p. 69.

TORTELLINI ALLA PANNA
Tortellini with Cream Sauce

1 lb./450 g. tortellini 1 1/2 tbsp./20 g. salt 4 quarts/4 L. cold water 1 tbsp./15 mL. oil	Add salt to water in a 5 quart/5 L. pot. Bring water to a boil on high heat and add tortellini. Cook al dente: 7-10 minutes for fresh pasta; 10-15 minutes for packaged or frozen tortellini. Drain and rinse with cold running water. Add oil to tortellini after draining and rinsing (the oil prevents the pasta sticking). Set aside.

Cream Sauce:

2 cups/450 mL. whipping cream	*Cook cream in a large skillet on medium heat until it begins to bubble.*
salt (to taste) freshly ground black pepper (to taste)	*Season with salt and pepper.*
	Add tortellini to cream. Toss and heat.
2 cups/450 g. Parmesan cheese, coarsely grated	*Gradually add Parmesan cheese to tortellini. Toss together and heat thoroughly until cheese melts and sauce thickens.*
1/2 cup/125 g. Parmesan cheese, coarsely grated 2 tsp./10 g. fresh parsley, finely chopped	*Put tortellini into a warm serving bowl or on warm plates. Sprinkle with Parmesan cheese and parsley and serve.*

This recipe for Tortellini alla Panna serves 4-6 people.

TORTELLINI BOLOGNESE
Tortellini with Meat Sauce

Meat Sauce:

3 cups/700 mL. meat sauce (see p. 34)	*Prepare the meat sauce first.*
	Prepare pasta 20 minutes before meat sauce is ready. Time your pasta so that it is done al dente at the same time as your sauce is ready.
1 lb./450 g. tortellini	*Cook al dente: 7-10 minutes for fresh pasta; 10-15 minutes for packaged or frozen tortellini (see p. 38). Drain, but do not rinse.*
1/4 cup/50 g. Parmesan cheese, coarsely grated	*Put tortellini into a warm serving bowl or on warm plates. Spoon meat sauce over tortellini, sprinkle with Parmesan cheese and serve.*

This recipe for Tortellini Bolognese serves 4-6 people.

TORTELLINI NAPOLETANA
Tortellini with Tomatoes

Tomato Sauce:

3 cups/700 mL. tomato sauce
(see p. 33)

Prepare the tomato sauce first.

*Prepare pasta 20 minutes before
tomato sauce is ready. Time your pasta
so that it is done al dente at the same time
as your sauce is ready.*

1 lb./450 g. tortellini

*Cook al dente: 7-10 minutes for fresh pasta;
10-15 minutes for packaged or frozen
tortellini (see p. 38).
Drain, but do not rinse.*

1/4 cup/50 g. Parmesan cheese,
coarsely grated
2 tsp./10 g. fresh parsley,
finely chopped

*Put tortellini into a warm serving bowl
or on warm plates.
Spoon tomato sauce over tortellini,
sprinkle with Parmesan cheese
and parsley and serve.*

This recipe for Tortellini Napoletana serves 4-6 people.

AGNOLOTTI CON RICOTTA E SPINACI
Agnolotti Stuffed with Ricotta Cheese and Spinach

18 fresh pasta squares,
cut 4 inches/10 cm. square

Stuffing:

2 bunches of fresh spinach

*Wash and stem spinach.
Discard any limp or discoloured leaves.*

3/4 cup/175 mL. cold water

*Steam spinach in boiling water in a
covered saucepan for 3-4 minutes, then
drain and rinse with cold running water.
Remove all water from spinach by
squeezing spinach by hand, then dry
with a clean cloth.
Finely chop spinach, then put in a bowl.*

1 cup/250 g. ricotta cheese
2 egg yolks
1/4 cup/50 g. Parmesan cheese,
coarsely grated
salt (to taste)
freshly ground black pepper (to taste)
1/8 tsp./pinch of nutmeg

*Add ricotta cheese, egg yolks, Parmesan
cheese, salt, pepper and nutmeg to spinach
in bowl and mix together very thoroughly
until almost a purée.*

	Lay uncooked pasta squares on a clean work surface and put approximately 1 tbsp./15 g. of stuffing in the centre of each pasta square.
1 egg a few drops of water	*Beat egg and a few drops of water in a bowl and brush the perimeter of each pasta square with egg.*
	Fold each pasta square in half from corner to corner to form a triangle and leaving the pasta on the surface, use the prongs of a fork to lightly press the open sides of the triangle closed and seal the stuffing in so that no water can enter.
1/4 cup/50 g. flour	*Put agnolotti, separated from one another, on a clean dry cloth that has been lightly dusted with flour.*
1 tbsp./15 mL. oil 1 1/2 tbsp./20 g. salt 4 quarts/4 L. cold water	*Add oil and salt to water in a 5 quart/5 L. pot (the oil prevents the pasta sticking). Bring water to a boil on high heat and add agnolotti.* *Cook al dente: 12-15 minutes.* *Drain and rinse with cold running water. Set aside.*
Cream Sauce:	
1 tbsp./15 g. butter	*Melt butter in a skillet on medium heat.*
2 cups/450 mL. whipping cream	*Add cream to butter and cook on medium heat until it begins to bubble.*
	Add agnolotti to cream and simmer on medium heat for 2-3 minutes.
1 cup/250 g. Parmesan cheese, coarsely grated	*Gradually add Parmesan cheese to agnolotti.* *Stir carefully with a wooden spoon, so as not to break the pasta, and heat until cheese melts and sauce thickens.*
salt (to taste) freshly ground black pepper (to taste)	*Season with salt and pepper.*
1/4 cup/50 g. Parmesan cheese, coarsely grated 2 tsp./10 g. fresh parsley, finely chopped	*Lift agnolotti from skillet and put into a warm serving bowl or on warm plates. Coat with sauce, sprinkle with Parmesan cheese and parsley and serve.*

This recipe for Agnolotti con Ricotta e Spinaci serves 4-6 people. Agnolotti con Ricotta e Spinaci is illustrated on p. 70.

AGNOLOTTI CON RIPIENO DI CARNE
Agnolotti Stuffed with Meat

18 fresh pasta squares,
cut 4 inches/10 cm. square

Stuffing:

2 tsp./10 g. butter 1/2 lb./250 g. lean ground beef	*Sauté ground beef in butter in a skillet on medium heat for 5 minutes until evenly brown, then put in a bowl.*
1/2 bunch of fresh spinach	*Wash and stem spinach.* *Discard any limp or discoloured leaves.*
3/4 cup/175 mL. cold water	*Steam spinach in boiling water in a covered saucepan for 2-3 minutes, then drain and rinse with cold running water. Remove all water from spinach by squeezing spinach by hand, then dry with a clean cloth.* *Finely chop spinach, then add to ground beef in bowl and mix together.*
1 tsp./5 mL. olive oil 1 tsp./5 g. butter 1 small onion, ground	*Sauté onion in oil and butter in another skillet on medium heat until onion is transparent.*
1 small carrot, ground 1 stalk celery, ground 1 clove garlic, finely chopped	*Add carrot, celery and garlic to onion and sauté on medium heat for 5 minutes.*
	Add onion, carrot, celery and garlic to ground beef and spinach in bowl and mix together.
1 egg 1/4 cup/50 mL. white sauce (see p. 32) 1/4 cup/50 g. Parmesan cheese, coarsely grated 2 tbsp./30 g. bread crumbs 2 tbsp./30 mL. dry red wine salt (to taste) freshly ground black pepper (to taste) 1/8 tsp./pinch of nutmeg	*Add egg, white sauce, Parmesan cheese, bread crumbs, wine, salt, pepper and nutmeg to ground beef, spinach, onion, carrot, celery and garlic and mix together thoroughly.*
	Lay uncooked pasta squares on a clean flat work surface and put approximately 1 tbsp./15 g. of stuffing in the centre of each pasta square.
1 egg a few drops of water	*Beat egg and a few drops of water in a bowl and brush the perimeter of each pasta square with egg.*

Fold each pasta square in half from
corner to corner to form a triangle
and leaving the pasta on the flat surface, use
the prongs of a fork to lightly press the
open sides of the triangle closed and seal
the stuffing in so that no water can enter.

1/4 cup/50 g. flour

Put agnolotti, separated from one
another, on a clean dry cloth that
has been lightly dusted with flour.

1 tbsp./15 mL. oil
1 1/2 tbsp./20 g. salt
4 quarts/4 L. cold water

Add oil and salt to water in a 5 quart/5 L.
pot (the oil prevents the pasta sticking).
Bring water to a boil on high heat
and add agnolotti.
Cook al dente: 12-15 minutes.
Drain, but do not rinse.

2 cups/450 mL. meat sauce
(see p. 34), warmed
1/4 cup/50 g. Parmesan cheese,
coarsely grated
2 tsp./10 g. fresh parsley,
finely chopped

Put agnolotti into a warm serving bowl
or on warm plates.
Spoon meat sauce over agnolotti,
sprinkle with Parmesan cheese
and parsley and serve.

This recipe for Agnolotti con Ripieno di Carne serves 4-6 people.

CANNELLONI DI MARE
Cannelloni Stuffed with Seafood and Spinach

Pre-heat oven to 350° F/180° C.

18 fresh pasta squares,
cut 4 inches/10 cm. square

Cook al dente: 3-5 minutes for fresh pasta
(see p. 38).

Stuffing:

1 lb./450 g. fresh crabmeat

Put crabmeat in a bowl.

2 bunches of fresh spinach

Wash and stem spinach.
Discard any limp or discoloured leaves.

3/4 cup/175 mL. cold water

Steam spinach in boiling water in a
covered saucepan for 3-4 minutes, then
drain and rinse with cold running water.
Remove all water from spinach by
squeezing spinach by hand, then dry
with a clean cloth.
Finely chop spinach, then add to
crabmeat in bowl and mix together.

(cont'd over)

Cont'd from page 81

1 tsp./5 mL. olive oil 1 tsp./5 g. butter 1 small onion, ground 2 cloves garlic, finely chopped	*Sauté onion and garlic in oil and butter in a skillet on medium heat until onion is transparent, then add to crabmeat and spinach in bowl and mix together.*
2 eggs 1 cup/250 mL. white sauce (see p. 32) 2 tbsp./30 g. bread crumbs salt (to taste) freshly ground black pepper (to taste) 1 tsp./5 g. fresh nutmeg, grated	*Add eggs, white sauce, bread crumbs, salt, pepper and nutmeg to crabmeat, spinach, onion and garlic in bowl and mix together thoroughly.*
	Put a portion of the stuffing on each pasta square and roll up.
1 cup/250 mL. whipping cream	*Cover the bottom of a casserole dish with cream and put cannelloni in dish, side by side.*
1 cup/250 mL. white sauce (see p. 32) 1 cup/250 g. Parmesan cheese, coarsely grated	*Cover cannelloni with white sauce and Parmesan cheese and put casserole dish in oven and bake at 350° F/180° C for 30 minutes until bubbling.*
	Serve on warm plates.

This recipe for Cannelloni di Mare makes 18 cannelloni. You can make this recipe ahead and freeze some of the cannelloni, but do not keep for too long. Use more pasta squares than necessary when cooking the pasta; some may tear in cooking.

CANNELLONI ALLA FIORENTINA
Cannelloni Stuffed with Meat and Spinach

	Pre-heat oven to 350° F/180° C.
30 fresh pasta squares, cut 4 inches/10 cm. square	*Cook al dente: 3-5 minutes for fresh pasta (see p. 38).*
Stuffing:	
1 tbsp./15 g. butter 3 lbs./1.5 kg. ground veal	*Sauté ground veal in butter in a large skillet on medium heat for 5 minutes until ground veal turns white, then put in a bowl.*
2 bunches of fresh spinach	*Wash and stem spinach. Discard any limp or discoloured leaves.*

3/4 cup/175 mL. cold water

Steam spinach in boiling water in a covered saucepan for 3-4 minutes, then drain and rinse with cold running water. Remove all water from spinach by squeezing spinach by hand, then dry with a clean cloth.
Finely chop spinach, then add to ground veal in bowl and mix together.

1 tsp./5 mL. olive oil
1 tsp./5 g. butter
1 large onion, ground

Sauté onion in oil and butter in another skillet on medium heat until onion is transparent.

1 large carrot, ground
2 stalks celery, ground
3 cloves garlic, finely chopped

Add carrot, celery and garlic to onion and sauté on medium heat for 5 minutes, then add onion, carrot, celery and garlic to ground veal and spinach in bowl and mix together.

4 eggs
1 cup/250 mL. white sauce
(see p. 32)
1 cup/250 g. Parmesan cheese, coarsely grated
1/4 cup/50 g. bread crumbs
salt (to taste)
freshly ground black pepper (to taste)
1/8 tsp./pinch of nutmeg

Add eggs, white sauce, Parmesan cheese, bread crumbs, salt, pepper and nutmeg to ground veal, spinach, onion, carrot, celery and garlic and mix together thoroughly.

Put a portion of the stuffing on each pasta square and roll up.

1 cup/250 mL. whipping cream

Cover the bottom of a casserole dish with cream and put cannelloni in dish, side by side.

2 cups/450 mL. white sauce
(see p. 32)
1 cup/250 g. Parmesan cheese, coarsely grated

Cover cannelloni with white sauce and Parmesan cheese and put casserole dish in oven and bake at 350° F/180° C for 30 minutes until bubbling.

Serve on warm plates.

This recipe for Cannelloni alla Fiorentina makes 30 cannelloni. Make this recipe ahead and freeze some of the cannelloni. Use more pasta squares than necessary when cooking the pasta; some may tear in cooking. Cannelloni alla Fiorentina is illustrated on p. 70.

LASAGNA AL FORNO
Baked Lasagna

Pre-heat oven to 300° F/150° C.

1 lb./450 g. fresh lasagna noodles
(or 1 1/2 lbs./700 g. if using packaged
lasagna)
1 tbsp./15 mL. oil
1 1/2 tbsp./20 g. salt
4 quarts/4 L. cold water

Add oil and salt to water in a 5 quart/5 L.
pot (the oil prevents the pasta sticking).
Bring water to a boil on high heat
and add lasagna noodles.
Cook al dente: 3-5 minutes for fresh pasta;
5-7 minutes for packaged lasagna.
Drain and rinse with cold running water.
Set aside.

2 tbsp./30 g. butter
1/4 cup/50 mL. white sauce
(see p. 32)

Spread butter and white sauce in the
bottom of a 16 x 12 x 3 inch/40 x 30 x 8 cm.
baking pan.

Put one layer of lasagna noodles on top of
butter and white sauce in pan.

4 cups/900 mL. meat sauce
(see p. 34)

Spread 1 cup/250 mL. of meat sauce on top
of lasagna noodles.

2 cups/450 mL. white sauce
(see p. 32)

Spread 1/2 cup/125 mL. of white sauce on
top of meat sauce.

2 cups/450 g. Parmesan cheese,
coarsely grated

Sprinkle 1/2 cup/125 g. of Parmesan cheese
on top of lasagna noodles, meat sauce and
white sauce.

Cover Parmesan cheese with another
layer of lasagna noodles.

Repeat until there are four layers,
ending with Parmesan cheese on top.

Put baking dish in oven and bake at
300° F/150° C for 30 minutes.

Serve on warm plates.

This recipe for Lasagna al Forno serves 6-8 people. Lasgna al Forno is illustrated on
p. 70.

GNOCCHI ALLA PIEMONTESE
Potato Dumplings with Meat Sauce

Pre-heat oven to 400° F/200° C.

3 lbs./1.5 kg. potatoes, peeled and quartered salt (to taste) cold water	*Add salt to water in a pot.* *Bring water to a boil on high heat and add potatoes.* *Cook potatoes until tender, then strain and mash.*
3 cups/700 g. flour	*Spread flour on a cutting board or flat work surface.* *While potatoes are still warm, add flour to potatoes to form a dough.* *Knead dough just until flour is well blended (if dough is handled too much, the gnocchi will be soggy and leaden).* *Flour hands and roll gnocchi into sausage shape about 1/2 inch/1 cm. in diameter, then cut into 1 inch/2.5 cm. pieces.* *Using thumb and index finger, pinch the centre of each gnocchi, then put them on a lightly floured cloth, careful so that they do not touch each other.*
salt (to taste) cold water	*Add salt to water in another pot.* *Bring water to a boil on high heat and drop gnocchi into water.* *As soon as gnocchi float to the surface, remove them with a slotted spoon.* *Drain gnocchi on a clean dry cloth.*
3 cups/700 mL. meat sauce (*see p. 34*), warmed 1/4 cup/50 g. butter 1/2 cup/125 g. Parmesan cheese, coarsely grated	*Put gnocchi in a casserole dish, then coat with meat sauce and sprinkle with butter and Parmesan cheese.*
	Put casserole dish in oven and bake at 400° F/200° C for 5-10 minutes.
1/2 cup/125 g. Parmesan cheese, coarsely grated	*Serve from casserole dish or put on warm plates.* *Sprinkle with Parmesan cheese before serving.*

This recipe for Gnocchi alla Piemontese serves 6-8 people.

Piatti Forti
Main Courses

The recipes in this section of the book are for main courses only. In most cases, they do *not* include suggestions as to what vegetables to serve with them. Again, the rule to follow is to serve whatever is available and fresh. In winter, you would serve: potatoes, onions, brussels sprouts or any of the root vegetables (carrots, turnip, parsnip or beets). In summer, try: peas, beans, asparagus, spinach, artichokes, eggplant, zucchini or squash. Tomatoes, broccoli and cauliflower can be served all year round, but do not serve broccoli with a Hollandaise Sauce if your main course is prepared with a butter-base sauce; or cauliflower with a cheese sauce if cheese is used in any quantity in the main course recipe. And do not serve scalloped potatoes cooked in cream if your main course has a cream-base sauce. Your vegetables should always compliment your entrée.

Most of the fish dishes which are accompanied with a sauce are best when served with boiled new potatoes or plain risotto (see p. 178) and fresh steamed vegetables—whatever is in season. For meat, fowl and game dishes, serve with small roast potatoes and root vegetables that have been lightly boiled, then tossed in butter. For most of the veal dishes, serve with a simple pasta tossed in butter and/or with cheese (if cheese is not used in the veal recipe) and whatever is available and fresh in the way of vegetables.

Most of the recipes in this section of the book have sauces which are made by deglazing the pan or skillet in which the fish, meat, fowl or game was cooked with cream, stock or wine. You should have chicken and beef consommé on hand, as well as fish and veal stock, if you are using this book often. Chicken and beef consommé (see pp. 19 and 20) and fish and veal stock (see pp. 30 and 31) can be made ahead and stored in your refrigerator or frozen in your freezer for up to two weeks. To deglaze is to swill a roasting pan or skillet with cream, stock or wine to pick up all the concentrated juices left in the pan or skillet after cooking fish, meat, fowl or game, to form the basis of the sauce to be prepared. Also used in this section are: tomato sauce and white sauce. You should have tomato sauce (see p. 33) on hand if you are using this book often—you will need it for many of the pasta recipes; white sauce (see p. 32), you can prepare at the time.

Buon appetito!

Illustration #7: Shellfish. *From left to right:* Cozze Marinara, Scampi alla Griglia and Zuppa di Vongole all' Italiana. Tiles courtesy of World Mosaic Ltd.; plates courtesy of Holt Renfrew.

Shellfish

ZUPPA DI VONGOLE ALL' ITALIANA
Steamed Clams in White Wine and Tomatoes

1 3/4-2 lbs./800 g.-1 kg. fresh clams	*Wash clams under cold running water to remove sand, then put them in a pot.*
1 tbsp./15 g. butter 1 large shallot, finely chopped 2 cloves garlic, finely chopped	*Sauté shallot and garlic in butter in a skillet on medium heat until shallot is transparent.*
2 large ripe tomatoes	*Blanch tomatoes by dropping them into a saucepan of boiling water until skin splits. Peel, seed and chop tomatoes. Add tomatoes to shallot and garlic and simmer on medium heat for approximately 2 minutes.*
salt (to taste) freshly ground black pepper (to taste) 1 bayleaf	*Season with salt, pepper and bayleaf.*
	Add shallots, garlic and tomatoes to clams in pot.
1 cup/250 mL. cold water 1 cup/250 mL. dry white wine	*Add water and wine to clams, shallot, garlic and tomatoes in pot, then cover pot, bring to a boil on high heat and steam clams for 7-10 minutes until their shells open.* *Some clams will not open; discard these.*
	Ladle clams and liquid into a warm soup tureen or into warm soup bowls.
1 tbsp./15 g. fresh parsley, finely chopped	*Sprinkle with parsley and serve.*

This recipe for Zuppa di Vongole all' Italiana serves 2 people. Zuppa di Vongole all' Italiana is illustrated on p. 87.

Illustration #8: Shellfish. *From left to right*: Granchio alla Veneziana, Granchio Mousseline and Ostriche alla Fiorentina. Tiles courtesy of World Mosaic Ltd.; plates courtesy of Holt Renfrew; serviette and serviette ring courtesy of Georg Jensen.

COZZE MARINARA
Mussels in White Wine, Cream and Onions

1 1/2-2 lbs./700 g.-1 kg. black mussels

Wash mussels with cold running water to remove sand, then set aside.

2 tbsp./30 g. butter
1 small onion, finely chopped

Sauté onion in butter in a large pot on medium heat until onion is transparent.

1 cup/250 mL. dry white wine
1 cup/250 mL. cold water

Add wine and water to onion in pot and stir until well blended.

salt (to taste)
freshly ground black pepper (to taste)
1 clove garlic, chopped
1 bayleaf, crushed

Season with salt, pepper, garlic and bayleaf.

Add mussels to onion, wine, water, salt, pepper, garlic and bayleaf in pot, then cover pot, bring to a boil on high heat and steam mussels for 2-3 minutes until their shells open.

1 cup/250 mL. whipping cream

Add cream to onion, wine, water, salt, pepper, garlic, bayleaf and mussels and stir until well blended.

juice of 1/2 lemon

Squeeze lemon juice directly into onion, wine, water, salt, pepper, garlic, bayleaf, mussels and cream and stir until well blended.

1 tbsp./15 g. fresh parsley, finely chopped

Add parsley to onion, wine, water, salt, pepper, garlic, bayleaf, mussels, cream and lemon juice, stir until well blended and simmer on medium heat for 2-3 minutes.

Ladle the mussels and liquid into a warm soup tureen or into warm soup bowls and serve.

This recipe for Cozze Marinara serves 2 people. Cozze Marinara is illustrated on p. 87.

OSTRICHE ALLA FIORENTINA
Oysters Florentine

Pre-heat the oven to 400° F/200° C.

12 fresh oysters in shell or 12 oz./350 g. shucked oysters	Put each oyster on the deepest side of oyster shell.

Spinach Mixture:

2 bunches of fresh spinach
cold water

Wash and stem spinach.
Discard any limp or discoloured leaves.
Blanch spinach by dropping it into a
saucepan of boiling water, then drain.
Finely chop spinach and put it in a bowl.

2 tbsp./30 g. butter
1 tbsp./15 g. onion, finely chopped

Sauté onion in butter in a skillet on
medium heat until onion is transparent,
then add to spinach in bowl.

1/4 cup/50 mL. white sauce
(*see p. 32*)

Add white sauce to spinach and onion
in bowl and mix together thoroughly.

salt (to taste)
freshly ground black pepper (to taste)
1/8 tsp./pinch of nutmeg

Season with salt, pepper and nutmeg.

Put a small amount of the spinach mixture
on the deepest side of each oyster shell
and put oyster on top of spinach mixture.

1 3/4 cups/400 mL. white sauce
(*see p. 32*)

Coat oyster and spinach mixture
with a small amount of white sauce.

1/4 cup/50 g. Parmesan cheese,
coarsely grated

Sprinkle Parmesan cheese on top of
oyster, spinach mixture and white sauce.

Put oysters on a baking sheet and put
baking sheet in oven and bake at
400° F/200° C for 15 minutes, then broil
for 2-3 minutes until cheese turns brown.

rock salt
1 lemon, cut into wedges
2 sprigs of fresh parsley

Preferably, put oysters on a bed of
rock salt.
Garnish with lemon wedges and sprigs
of parsley and serve.

This recipe for Ostriche alla Fiorentina serves 2 people. Ostriche alla Fiorentina is illustrated on p. 88.

GAMBERONI AFFINOCCHIATI
Prawns with Anise

1 lb./450 g. fresh prawns,
peeled and cleaned

Sauce:

2 tbsp./30 g. butter	*Sauté prawns in butter in a skillet on medium heat for 3 minutes, turning them occasionally.*
2 tbsp./30 mL. Pernod	*Add Pernod to prawns and reduce by simmering on medium heat for 2-3 minutes.*
1/2 cup/125 mL. whipping cream	*Add cream to prawns and Pernod and cook on medium heat until cream begins to bubble.*
salt (to taste) freshly ground black pepper (to taste)	*Season with salt and pepper.*
juice of 1/2 lemon	*Squeeze lemon juice directly into prawns, Pernod and cream and stir until well blended.*
1 tsp./5 g. fresh parsley, finely chopped	*Put prawns on a warm serving platter or on warm plates. Coat with sauce, sprinkle with parsley and serve.*

This recipe for Gamberoni Affinocchiati serves 2 people. Gamberoni are illustrated on the cover.

SCAMPI ALLA GRIGLIA
Broiled Baby Lobster Tail

Pre-heat oven to 400° F/200° C.

1 lb./450 g. Icelandic scampi
salt (to taste)
freshly ground black pepper (to taste)
1/8 tsp./pinch of paprika (for colour)

Cut scampi in half lengthwise with a sharp knife, but leave them in the shell. Put scampi in a shallow casserole dish and season with salt, pepper and paprika.

1/4 cup/50 g. butter
1 clove garlic, finely chopped

Put a small amount of butter on each scampi and sprinkle with garlic.

Put casserole dish in oven and bake at 400° F/200° C for 5 minutes, then broil for 2 minutes.
Remove scampi from casserole dish and keep warm.

Sauce:

1/4 cup/50 mL. dry white wine

Add wine to casserole dish and reduce by simmering on medium heat for 2-3 minutes.

juice of 1/2 lemon

Squeeze lemon juice directly into wine and stir until well blended.

1 tbsp./15 g. fresh parsley, finely chopped

Add parsley to wine and lemon juice and stir until well blended.

1/2 lemon, cut in wedges
2 sprigs of fresh parsley

Put scampi on a warm serving platter or on warm plates.
Coat with sauce, garnish with lemon wedges and sprigs of parsley and serve.

This recipe for Scampi alla Griglia serves 2 people. Scampi alla Griglia is illustrated on p. 87.

GRANCHIO ALLA VENEZIANA
Crab Stuffed with Shrimp and Spinach

Pre-heat oven to 400° F/200° C.

3 (1 1/2 lb./700 g.) whole fresh Dungeness crab

Put crab in a large pot.

1 lemon, peeled and sliced
1 stalk celery and celery top, chopped
1 tbsp./15 g. salt
8-10 peppercorns
1 bayleaf
cold water

Add lemon, celery, salt, peppercorns, bayleaf and enough water to cover crab in pot, then bring water to a boil on high heat and boil crab for approximately 5 minutes.

Remove crab from water and allow to cool.
Remove shells from crab; scrape away entrails and discard them.
Rinse shells well with cold running water. Remove crabmeat from body using a fine knife or a nut pick (for the crab stuffing, you will need a total of 6 oz./175 g. of crabmeat).
The meat taken from the body of the three crab will not give you this amount.
Therefore, use the meat from 3-4 crab legs from the third crab.
Once crabmeat is extracted from crab, finely chop and put in a bowl.

3/4 cup/175 g. fresh baby shrimp
1/2 tsp./2 g. fresh parsley, finely chopped
1/8 tsp./pinch of fresh basil, finely chopped
white pepper (to taste)
1 cup/250 mL. white sauce (see p. 32)
2 tbsp./30 g. Parmesan cheese, coarsely grated

Add shrimp, parsley, basil, pepper, white sauce and Parmesan cheese to crabmeat in bowl and mix together thoroughly, then set aside.

1 bunch of fresh spinach

Wash and stem spinach.
Discard any limp or discoloured leaves.

3/4 cup/175 mL. cold water

Steam spinach in boiling water in a covered saucepan for 3-4 minutes, then drain and rinse with cold running water. Remove all water from spinach by squeezing spinach by hand, then dry with a clean cloth.
Finely chop spinach and set aside.

2 tsp./10 g. butter 1 small onion, finely chopped	*Sauté onion in butter in a skillet on medium heat for approximately 1 minute.*
1 clove garlic, finely chopped	*Add spinach and garlic to onion and sauté on medium heat for another 2-3 minutes.*
salt (to taste) white pepper (to taste) 1/8 tsp./pinch of nutmeg	*Season with salt, pepper and nutmeg.*
	Add onion, spinach and garlic to crabmeat, shrimp, parsley, basil, pepper, white sauce and Parmesan cheese and mix together thoroughly, then fill 2 crab shells with this mixture.
1 tsp./5 g. butter 1/4 cup/50 g. Parmesan cheese, coarsely grated	*Sprinkle butter and Parmesan cheese on top of crab mixture in shells.*
butter	*Put crab shells on a buttered baking sheet, arrange claws and legs around shells and put baking sheet in oven and bake at 400° F/200° C for 10 minutes or until stuffing is thoroughly heated.*
lemon butter (see below)	*Put crab shells surrounded by crab claws and legs on warm plates and serve with lemon butter on the side.*

Lemon Butter:

1/2 cup/125 g. butter	*Melt butter in a skillet on medium heat.*
juice of 1 lemon	*Squeeze lemon juice directly into butter and stir until well blended.*
2 tsp./10 g. fresh parsley, finely chopped	*Add parsley to butter and lemon juice and stir until well blended.*

This recipe for Granchio alla Veneziana serves 2 people. Granchio alla Veneziana is illustrated on p. 88.

ALASKA KING CRAB LEGS VIAREGGIO
Alaska King Crab Legs in Bernaise Sauce

Pre-heat oven to 400° F/200° C.

3 lbs./1.5 kg. fresh or frozen crab legs, split in half

Put crab legs in a bowl of cold water to thaw if frozen and rinse under cold running water to remove salt.
Put crab legs on a clean dry cloth and pat dry, then put in a baking dish.

1 cup/250 mL. dry white wine
2 tbsp./30 g. butter
1/2 tsp./2 g. white pepper

Pour wine over crab legs, then dab crab legs with butter.
Season with pepper.

Put baking dish in oven and bake at 400° F/200° C for 10 minutes.

1 cup/250 mL. Bernaise sauce (see below)

Remove baking dish from oven and lightly coat crab legs with Bernaise sauce.

Return baking dish to oven and broil crab legs for 20-30 seconds to lightly brown the Bernaise sauce.

1/2 lemon, cut into wedges
2 sprigs of fresh parsley

Arrange crab legs on a warm serving platter or on warm plates.
Garnish with lemon wedges and sprigs of parsley and serve.

Bernaise Sauce:

3 tbsp./45 mL. tarragon vinegar
4 tbsp./60 mL. dry white wine
1 tbsp./15 g. shallot, finely chopped
1/2 tsp./2 g. fresh chervil, finely chopped
1/8 tsp./pinch of fresh tarragon, finely chopped
1/8 tsp./pinch of black peppercorns, crushed

Mix vinegar, wine, shallot, chervil, tarragon and crushed peppercorns together in a pot, bring to a boil on high heat and reduce by one-half.

Strain herb mixture into a bowl through a sieve lined with a linen or muslin cloth, separating the herbs from the liquid.
Discard herbs and allow the liquid to cool.

4 egg yolks	*Beat egg yolks and water in the top half*
2 tbsp./30 mL. cold water	*of a double boiler, but do not place over*
	boiling water.

Slowly add cooled liquid to egg yolks and water, then place over boiling water and whip constantly until the mixture becomes fluffy.

1 cup/250 g. butter, melted	*Remove top half of double boiler from heat and slowly add melted butter to mixture, whisking constantly.*
	Whisk until all the butter is used up and has been absorbed into the mixture.

1/8 tsp./pinch of fresh parsley, finely chopped
1/8 tsp./pinch of fresh chervil, finely chopped
1/8 tsp./pinch of fresh tarragon, finely chopped
salt (to taste)

Add parsley, chervil, tarragon and salt to mixture and whisk to evenly distribute.

Keep sauce over the warm water of the double boiler and serve warm.

This recipe for Alaska King Crab Legs Viareggio serves 2 people. The recipe for Bernaise Sauce yields approximately 1 cup/250 mL..

GRANCHIO MOUSSELINE
Crab Mousseline

Pre-heat oven to 400° F/200° C.

1 1/2 lbs./700 g. crabmeat

Marinade:

1 cup/250 mL. dry white wine
2 tbsp./30 g. shallot, finely chopped
2 tbsp./30 g. fresh tarragon, finely chopped

Mix wine, shallot and tarragon together in a bowl.

Add crabmeat to marinade and refrigerate for 2 hours, then drain.

Put crabmeat in a blender or food processor and chop very fine.

5 egg whites

Add egg whites one at a time to crabmeat in blender or food processor and mix for 30 seconds per egg white.

salt (to taste)
white pepper (to taste)
1/8 tsp./pinch of mace

Season with salt, pepper and mace.

3 1/2 cups/800 mL. whipping cream

Gradually add cream to crabmeat and egg whites and mix until cream is well blended.

2 tsp./10 g. butter
2 crab claws

Butter the bottom of 4 ramekins and extract the crabmeat from 2 crab claws.

Put crabmeat from claws on the bottom of each ramekin and fill ramekins with crab mixture.

Cover ramekins with foil and put ramekins in a pan of water in oven and bake at 400° F/200° C for 25 minutes.

1 large ripe tomato

Blanch tomato by dropping it into a saucepan of boiling water until skin splits. Peel, seed and chop tomato.

burro bianco
(see p. 99)
3-4 tbsp./45-60 g. fresh chives, finely chopped

Turn crab mousseline out on warm plates from ramekins.
Circle with burro bianco, then circle with chives, then circle with chopped tomato, and serve.

Burro Bianco:

1/2 cup/125 mL. fish stock
(*see p. 30*)
1/2 cup/125 mL. white wine vinegar
2 tsp./10 g. shallot,
finely chopped

Mix *fish stock, vinegar and shallot together in a pot and slowly bring to a boil on medium heat, then reduce by one-half by simmering on medium heat for 5-10 minutes until fish stock thickens slightly and becomes velvety.*

1/2 cup/125 g. butter, softened

Gradually add softened butter to fish stock, vinegar and shallot and whisk constantly in the same direction until butter is well blended.

This recipe for Crab Mousseline serves 4 people. Crab Mousseline is illustrated on p. 88.

CALAMARI FRITTI
Pan Fried Squid

3 lbs./1.5 kg. squid
salt (to taste)
freshly ground black pepper (to taste)
1 cup/250 g. flour

*Clean squid by pulling off the head
and pulling out the entrails.
Lay squid on a cutting board or flat surface
and using a sharp knife, scrape the skin off.
Wash squid thoroughly in cold running
water.
Cut off tentacles and make sure that
the beak-like mouth is discarded.
Chop tentacles and body into 1/2 inch/
1 cm. pieces.
Pat squid dry with a cloth or paper towel.
Season squid with salt and pepper.
Lightly flour, shaking off the excess.*

2 cups/450 mL. vegetable oil

*Fry squid in hot oil in a large skillet
on high heat for approximately 1 minute
until golden.
Do not overcrowd squid in skillet.
Drain squid on a cloth or paper towel.*

1 lemon, cut in wedges

*Put squid on a warm serving platter
or on warm plates.
Garnish with lemon wedges and serve.*

This recipe for Calamari Fritti serves 6 people.

CALAMARI RIPIENI
Stuffed Squid

Pre-heat oven to 375° F/190° C.

3 lbs./1.5 kg. squid

Clean squid (see p. 100) and cut off tentacles, making sure that the beak-like mouth is discarded.
Save tentacles.

Stuffing:

1 oz./25 g. prosciutto

Finely chop squid tentacles and prosciutto and put in a bowl.

1/4 cup/50 mL. olive oil
1 tsp./5 mL. tomato purée
1 tbsp./15 g. onion, finely chopped
2 cloves garlic, finely chopped
2 tbsp./30 g. fresh parsley, finely chopped
1 egg
2 tbsp./30 g. bread crumbs
1 tsp./5 g. salt
freshly ground black pepper (to taste)

Add oil, tomato purée, onion, garlic, parsley, egg, bread crumbs, salt and pepper to squid tentacles and prosciutto in bowl and mix together thoroughly.
Put stuffing in a piping bag.

Fill squid bodies with stuffing and seal both ends with a toothpick.

salt (to taste)
freshly ground black pepper (to taste)

Season squid with salt and pepper.

1/4 cup/50 g. flour

Lightly flour, shaking off the excess.

1/4 cup/50 mL. olive oil

Sauté squid in hot oil in a skillet on medium heat for 2-3 minutes until lightly coloured.

1/2 cup/125 mL. dry white wine or dry white vermouth

Put squid in a casserole dish and pour wine or vermouth over squid.

Put casserole dish in oven and bake at 375° F/190° C for 30 minutes.

Put squid on a warm serving platter or on warm plates and serve.

This recipe for Calamari Ripieni serves 6 people.

SOGLIOLA AL VINO ROSSO
Sole in Red Wine Sauce

2 (5-6 oz./150-175 g.) fillets of sole
salt (to taste)
freshly ground black pepper (to taste)
1/4 cup/50 g. flour

*Season sole with salt and pepper.
Lightly flour, shaking off the excess.*

1 tbsp./15 mL. olive oil
1 tbsp./15 g. butter

*Sauté sole on both sides in hot oil and
butter in a skillet on medium heat for 2-3
minutes per side (depending on thickness).
Remove sole from skillet and keep warm;
discard excess oil and butter from skillet.*

Sauce:

1/3 cup/75 mL. dry red wine

Deglaze skillet with wine.

1 tbsp./15 g. butter
1 tsp./5 g. fresh parsley,
finely chopped

*Add butter and parsley to wine
and reduce by one-half by simmering
on medium heat.*

1/2 lemon, cut in wedges
2 sprigs of fresh parsley

*Put sole on a warm serving platter
or on warm plates.
Coat with sauce, garnish with lemon
wedges and sprigs of parsley and serve.*

This recipe for Sogliola al Vino Rosso serves 2 people.

FILETTI DI SOGLIOLA AL VINO BIANCO CON CREMA
Fillet of Sole in White Wine, Cream, Mushrooms and Tomatoes

Pre-heat oven to 400° F/200° C.

4 (3 oz./85 g.) fillets of sole
salt (to taste)
freshly ground black pepper (to taste)
2 tsp./10 g. fresh parsley,
finely chopped

Season sole with salt and pepper.
Put 1/2 tsp./2 g. of parsley on each fillet
of sole and roll up.
Put sole in a shallow casserole dish,
side by side.

1 large ripe tomato

Blanch tomato by dropping it into a
saucepan of boiling water until skin splits.
Peel, seed and dice tomato.
Sprinkle tomato on top of sole.

2 mushrooms, sliced

Sprinkle mushrooms on top of sole
and tomato.

1/4 cup/50 mL. dry white wine
1/2 cup/125 mL. whipping cream

Mix wine and cream together in a bowl
and pour over sole, tomato and
mushrooms.

Put casserole dish, partly covered in foil,
in oven and bake at 400° F/200° C for
5 minutes.
Do not overcook.
Gently remove sole from casserole dish,
so that it does not break, and keep warm.

Sauce:

Bring tomato, mushrooms, wine and
cream left in casserole dish to a boil
on high heat, then reduce by simmering
on medium heat for 2-3 minutes.

1 egg yolk
1/4 cup/50 mL. whipping cream

Beat egg yolk in a bowl, then add cream
and mix together.

Slowly add egg yolk and cream to
tomato, mushrooms, wine and cream,
stir until well blended and simmer on
medium heat for 2-3 minutes until
sauce thickens slightly.

salt (to taste)
freshly ground black pepper (to taste)
1/8 tsp./pinch of paprika (for colour)

Put sole on a warm serving platter
or on warm plates.
Coat with sauce, season with salt, pepper
and paprika and serve.

This recipe for Filetti di Sogliola al Vino Bianco con Crema serves 2 people.

SOGLIOLA ALLA MUGNAIA
Dover Sole in Lemon Butter

Pre-heat oven to 375° F/190° C.

2 (1 lb./450 g.) Dover sole—
weight given is for uncleaned fish
with the head and tail left on
salt (to taste)
freshly ground black pepper (to taste)
1/4 cup/50 g. flour

*Clean and skin sole; trim fins from sides
and cut off head. We recommend
you have the fish market do this.
Season sole with salt and pepper.
Lightly flour, shaking off the excess.*

1/4 cup/50 mL. vegetable oil
2 tbsp./30 g. butter

*Sauté sole in hot oil and butter
in an ovenproof skillet or shallow
casserole dish on medium heat for 2-3
minutes per side (depending on thickness).*

*Put skillet or casserole dish, uncovered,
in oven and bake at 375° F/190° C
for 10 minutes.
To test: make a small slice at the thickest
part of the fish. If there is still blood on
the bone, bake for another 1-2 minutes.
Remove sole from skillet or casserole dish
and keep warm; discard excess oil and
butter from skillet or casserole dish.*

Lemon Butter:

1/4 cup/50 g. butter

*Melt butter in skillet or casserole dish on
medium heat until it turns golden brown.*

juice of 1/2 lemon

*Squeeze lemon juice directly into butter
and stir until well blended.*

1/2 lemon, cut in wedges
2 sprigs of fresh parsley

*Put sole on a warm serving platter
or on warm plates.
Pour lemon butter over sole, garnish with
lemon wedges and sprigs of parsley
and serve.*

This recipe for Sogliola alla Mugnaia serves 2 people.

Illustration #9: Fish. *Foreground*: Cioppino. *Background*: Grilse al Burro Bianco. Tiles courtesy of World Mosaic Ltd.; serving bowl and tray and serviette and serviette ring courtesy of The Patio Gallery.

COD PIZZAIOLA
Cod with Tomatoes, Garlic and Basil

2 (6-8 oz./175-250 g.) fillets of cod
salt (to taste)
freshly ground black pepper (to taste)

Season cod with salt and pepper.

2 cups/450 mL. cold water
2 tbsp./30 mL. dry white wine
juice of 1/2 lemon

Put water, wine and lemon juice in a large skillet and bring to a boil on high heat, then reduce heat slightly and steam cod for 5-6 minutes.

Remove cod from skillet and keep warm; discard water, wine and lemon juice.

Sauce:

1 cup/250 mL. tomato sauce
(see p. 33)
2 tbsp./30 mL. dry white wine
1 tsp./5 g. fresh basil,
finely chopped
1 tsp./5 g. fresh oregano,
finely chopped

Mix tomato sauce, wine, basil and oregano together in skillet and simmer on medium heat.

Add cod to tomato sauce, wine, basil and oregano and cook on medium heat for 3 minutes, basting the cod with the tomato sauce, wine, basil and oregano.

1 tbsp./15 g. black olives,
drained and sliced
2 tsp./10 g. fresh parsley,
finely chopped

Put cod on a warm serving platter or on warm plates.
Coat with sauce, garnish with olive slices, sprinkle with parsley and serve.

This recipe for Cod Pizzaiola serves 2 people. Cod Pizzaiola is illustrated on the page opposite.

Illustration #10: Fish. From left to right: Salmone Cetriolato, Cod Pizzaiola (upper plate) and Red Snapper al Vino Rosso (lower plate). Tiles courtesy of World Mosaic Ltd.; plates courtesy of Holt Renfrew.

HALIBUT ALLA GENOVESE
Halibut in a Light Green Sauce

2 (6 oz./175 g.) fillets of halibut
salt (to taste)
freshly ground black pepper (to taste)
1/4 cup/50 g. flour

Season halibut with salt and pepper.
Lightly flour, shaking off the excess.

1/4 cup/50 g. butter

Sauté halibut on both sides in hot butter
in a skillet on high heat until brown,
then reduce heat and sauté on medium
heat for approximately 5 minutes.
Remove halibut from skillet and
keep warm.

Sauce:

1/4 cup/50 mL. dry white wine

Deglaze skillet with wine.

juice of 1 lemon

Squeeze lemon juice directly into wine,
stir until well blended and reduce by
simmering on medium heat for
2-3 minutes.

1/2 cup/125 mL. whipping cream

Add cream to wine and lemon juice,
stir until well blended and reduce by
one-half by simmering on medium heat.

1 tbsp./15 mL. capers, drained
1 tsp./5 g. fresh parsley,
finely chopped
1/2 tsp./2 g. fresh basil,
finely chopped

Add capers, parsley and basil to wine,
lemon juice and cream and stir until
well blended.

salt (to taste)
freshly ground black pepper (to taste)

Season with salt and pepper.

Put halibut on a warm serving platter
or on warm plates.
Coat with sauce and serve.

This recipe for Halibut alla Genovese serves 2 people.

HALIBUT NAPOLETANA
Halibut with a Purée of Tomatoes and Clams

2 (5-6 oz./150-175 g.) fillets of halibut salt (to taste) freshly ground black pepper (to taste) 1/4 cup/50 g. flour	Season halibut with salt and pepper. Lightly flour, shaking off the excess.

Sauce (prepare sauce first):

1 tbsp./15 g. butter 1 small shallot, finely chopped 1 tbsp./15 g. celery, finely chopped 1 clove garlic, finely chopped 1/2 tsp./2 g. fresh basil, finely chopped	Sauté shallot, celery, garlic and basil in butter in a skillet on medium heat until shallot is transparent.
juice of 1/2 lemon 2 tbsp./30 mL. dry white wine	Add lemon juice and wine to shallot, celery, garlic and basil, stir until well blended and reduce by simmering on medium heat for 1-2 minutes.
2 large ripe tomatoes	Blanch tomatoes by dropping them into a saucepan of boiling water until skin splits. Peel, seed and chop tomatoes. Set aside.
1 lb./450 g. fresh clams	Wash clams with cold running water to remove sand, then put them in a pot.
2 tbsp./30 mL. dry white wine cold water	Add wine and enough water to cover the bottom of pot, then cover pot, bring to a boil on high heat and steam clams for 7-10 minutes until their shells open. Some clams will not open; discard these. Drain pot and remove clams from shells.
	Add tomatoes and clams to shallot, celery, garlic, basil, lemon juice and wine in skillet and simmer on medium heat for approximately 5 minutes.
salt (to taste) freshly ground black pepper (to taste)	Season with salt and pepper.
1 tbsp./15 mL. olive oil 1 tbsp./15 g. butter	Sauté halibut on both sides in hot oil and butter in another skillet on medium heat for 4-5 minutes per side (depending on thickness).
1/2 lemon, cut in wedges 2 leaves of fresh basil	Put halibut on a warm serving platter or on warm plates. Coat with sauce, garnish with lemon wedges and basil leaves and serve.

This recipe for Halibut Napoletana serves 2 people.

RED SNAPPER AL VINO ROSSO
Red Snapper in Red Wine with Abalone

Pre-heat oven to 350° F/180° C.

2 (6 oz./175 g.) fillets of red snapper
salt (to taste)
freshly ground black pepper (to taste)
2 tbsp./30 g. flour

Season red snapper with salt and pepper. Lightly flour, shaking off the excess.

2 tbsp./30 g. butter

Sauté red snapper in hot butter in a skillet on medium heat for 2 minutes per side. Remove red snapper from skillet and put in a small buttered baking pan.

Sauce:

1/4 cup/50 mL. dry red wine

Deglaze skillet with wine.

1/4 cup/50 mL. fish stock
(see p. 30)

Add fish stock to wine, stir until well blended and simmer on medium heat for approximately 1 minute.

Pour wine and fish stock over red snapper in baking pan and put pan in oven and bake at 350° F/180° C for 15 minutes.

1 abalone

Remove abalone from its shell — remove body and entrails, leaving only the foot of the abalone.
Trim off all the black from abalone and cut into thin slices.
Lightly pound abalone slices, then julienne.

1 tsp./5 g. butter

Sauté abalone in butter in another skillet on medium heat for approximately 1 minute.

Time the abalone so that it is done at the same time as red snapper is ready.

Put red snapper on a warm serving platter or on warm plates.

2 tbsp./30 g. butter

Add butter to wine and fish stock in baking pan and stir until well blended.

a few drops of lemon juice

Add lemon juice to wine, fish stock and butter and stir until well blended.

salt (to taste)
freshly ground black pepper (to taste)

Season with salt and pepper.

1 tsp./5 g. fresh parsley,
finely chopped

Put abalone strips on top of red snapper. Coat with sauce, sprinkle with parsley and serve.

STORIONE DELLA CANTINA
Sturgeon with Avocado

1 (12 oz./350 g.) fillet of sturgeon, cut 1/2 inch/1 cm. thick salt (to taste) freshly ground black pepper (to taste) 1/4 cup/50 g. flour	*Season sturgeon with salt and pepper. Lightly flour, shaking off the excess.*
1 tbsp./15 g. butter	*Pan fry sturgeon in hot butter in a skillet on medium heat for 7-10 minutes (depending on thickness). Remove sturgeon from skillet and keep warm.*
Sauce:	
	Time your sauce so that it is ready at the same time as sturgeon is done.
1 tsp./5 g. shallot, finely chopped	*Sauté shallot in skillet on medium heat until shallot is transparent.*
1/4 cup/50 g. avocado, diced small 1/4 cup/50 g. tomato, peeled and chopped small	*Add avocado and tomato to shallot and sauté on medium heat for approximately 2 minutes.*
1/4 cup/50 mL. dry white wine	*Add wine to shallot, avocado and tomato and reduce by simmering on medium heat for 2-3 minutes.*
1/4 cup/50 mL. whipping cream	*Add cream to shallot, avocado, tomato and wine, stir until well blended and cook on medium heat until cream begins to bubble.*
salt (to taste) freshly ground black pepper (to taste)	*Season with salt and pepper.*
1/2 lemon, cut in wedges	*Put sturgeon on a warm serving platter or on warm plates. Coat with sauce, garnish with lemon wedges and serve.*

This recipe for Storione della Cantina serves 2 people. The recipe for Red Snapper al Vino Rosso on p. 110 also serves 2 people. Red Snapper al Vino Rosso is illustrated on p. 106.

GRILSE AL BURRO BIANCO
Baby Salmon in Burro Bianco

Pre-heat oven to 375° F/190° C.

2 (6-8 oz./175-250 g.) baby salmon, filleted, but with the head, tail and skin left on
salt (to taste)
white pepper (to taste)
1/4 cup/50 g. flour

Season salmon inside and out with salt and pepper.
Lightly flour, shaking off the excess.

1/2 lemon, thinly sliced

Put lemon slices inside salmon.

2 tsp./10 mL. olive oil
2 tsp./10 g. butter

Sauté salmon in hot oil and butter in an ovenproof skillet on medium heat for approximately 1 minute per side— for colour.

Put skillet in oven and bake at 375° F/190° C for 8-10 minutes until salmon is done.

Burro Bianco:

1/4 cup/50 mL. fish stock (see p. 30)
1/4 cup/50 mL. white wine vinegar
1 tsp./5 g. shallot, finely chopped

Mix fish stock, vinegar and shallot together in a saucepan and slowly bring to a boil on medium heat, then reduce by one-half by simmering on medium heat for 5-10 minutes until fish stock thickens slightly and becomes velvety.

1/4 cup/50 g. butter, softened

Gradually add softened butter to fish stock, vinegar and shallot and whisk constantly in the same direction until butter is well blended.

2 sprigs of fresh parsley
1/8 tsp./pinch of paprika (for colour)

Put salmon on a warm serving platter or on warm plates.
Coat with burro bianco, garnish with sprigs of parsley, sprinkle with paprika and serve.

This recipe for Grilse al Burro Bianco serves 2 people. Grilse al Burro Bianco is illustrated on p. 105.

SALMONE AFFINOCCHIATO
Salmon in Fennel Sauce

2 (6-8 oz./175-250 g.) fillets of salmon salt (to taste) white pepper (to taste) 1 tsp./5 g. fennel seeds, crushed 1/4 cup/50 g. flour	Season salmon with salt, pepper and fennel seeds. Lightly flour, shaking off the excess.
1 tsp./5 mL. olive oil 1 tsp./5 g. butter	Sauté salmon in hot oil and butter in a skillet on medium heat for approximately 2 minutes per side. Remove salmon from skillet and keep warm; discard excess oil and butter from skillet.

Fennel Sauce:

1/4 cup/50 mL. dry white wine or dry white vermouth	Deglaze skillet with wine or vermouth.
juice of 1 lemon	Squeeze lemon juice directly into wine or vermouth and reduce by simmering on medium heat for 2-3 minutes.
1/3 cup/75 mL. whipping cream 1 tsp./5 g. fresh parsley, finely chopped	Add cream and parsley to wine or vermouth and lemon juice, stir until well blended and reduce by simmering on medium heat until sauce is thick enough to coat the back of a spoon.
salt (to taste) white pepper (to taste)	Season with salt and pepper.
4-6 leaves of fresh fennel	Put salmon on a warm serving platter or on warm plates. Coat with sauce, garnish with fennel leaves and serve.

This recipe for Salmone Affinocchiato serves 2 people.

SALMONE CETRIOLATO
Salmon with Cucumber

Pre-heat oven to 400° F/200° C.

2 (6-8 oz./175-250 g.) fillets of salmon
salt (to taste)
white pepper (to taste)
1/4 cup/50 g. flour

Season salmon with salt and pepper.
Lightly flour, shaking off the excess.

1 tbsp./15 mL. olive oil
1 tbsp./15 g. butter

Sauté salmon in hot oil and butter
in an ovenproof skillet on medium heat
for approximately 2 minutes per side.

1/4 cup/50 g. cucumber,
peeled and sliced 1/4 inch/.5 cm. thick

Put cucumber slices on top of salmon.

Put skillet, uncovered, in oven and
bake at 400° F/200° C for 5-6 minutes.
Remove salmon from skillet and keep
warm; discard excess oil and butter
from skillet.

Sauce:

1/4 cup/50 mL. dry white wine
or dry white vermouth

Deglaze skillet with wine or vermouth.

juice of 1/2 lemon

Squeeze lemon juice directly into wine
or vermouth and reduce by simmering
on medium heat for 2-3 minutes.

1/2 cup/125 mL. whipping cream

Add cream to wine or vermouth and
lemon juice and reduce by simmering on
medium heat until sauce is thick enough
to coat the back of a spoon.

1 tsp./5 g. fresh parsley,
finely chopped

Add parsley to wine or vermouth,
lemon juice and cream and stir until
well blended.

salt (to taste)
white pepper (to taste)

Season with salt and pepper.

2 sprigs of fresh dill
or 2 leaves of fresh fennel

Put salmon on a warm serving platter
or on warm plates.
Coat with sauce, garnish with sprigs
of dill or fennel leaves and serve.

This recipe for Salmone Cetriolato serves 2 people. Salmone Cetriolato is illustrated on p. 106.

SALMONE CON ACCIUGHE
Salmon with Anchovy Sauce

2 (6-8 oz./175-250 g.) fillets of salmon

2 tbsp./30 mL. dry white wine
cold water
2-3 onion rings
salt (to taste)
2-3 peppercorns
1 bayleaf

Put wine and enough water to barely cover salmon in skillet, then add onion rings, salt, pepper and bayleaf and bring to a boil on high heat.

Add salmon to wine, water, onion rings, salt, pepper and bayleaf in skillet and poach on medium heat for 5-6 minutes until salmon is done.
It is better to undercook salmon than overcook it.

Anchovy Sauce:

2 anchovy fillets, washed and pounded

Put anchovy fillets in another skillet.

1/4 cup/50 g. butter, softened

Add softened butter to anchovy fillets and stir until well blended.

1 cup/250 mL. white sauce
(see p. 32), thin consistency

Add white sauce to anchovy fillets and butter, stir until well blended and simmer on medium heat until sauce is thick enough to coat the back of a spoon.
If sauce is too thick, add milk.

1 small ripe tomato

Blanch tomato by dropping it into a saucepan of boiling water until skin splits. Peel, seed and chop tomato.
Set aside.

Put salmon on a warm serving platter or on warm plates.
Coat with sauce, garnish with chopped tomato and serve.

This recipe for Salmone con Acciughe serves 2 people.

CIOPPINO
Fish Stew

2 tbsp./30 mL. olive oil
2 tbsp./30 g. butter
1 large onion, finely chopped
5 cloves garlic, finely chopped

Sauté onion and garlic in oil and butter in a 5 quart/5 L. pot on medium heat until onion is transparent.

6 large ripe tomatoes

Blanch tomatoes by dropping them into a saucepan of boiling water until skin splits. Peel, seed and chop tomatoes.
Add tomatoes to onion and garlic in pot and sauté on medium heat for 1-2 minutes.

2 cups/450 mL. dry white wine
4 cups/900 mL. cold water

Add wine and water to onion, garlic and tomatoes and bring to a boil on high heat, then simmer on medium heat for 5 minutes, stirring frequently.

2 tsp./10 g. fresh basil, finely chopped
1 tbsp./15 g. fresh parsley, finely chopped
1 tsp./5 g. fresh oregano
1 tsp./5 g. fresh thyme
2 bayleaves, crushed
4 anchovy fillets, washed, dried and chopped
juice of 1 lemon

Mix basil, parsley, oregano, thyme, bayleaves, anchovies and lemon juice together in a bowl and stir until well blended.

Add basil, parsley, oregano, thyme, bayleaves, anchovies and lemon juice to onion, garlic, tomatoes, wine and water and stir until well blended.

salt (to taste)
freshly ground black pepper (to taste)

Season with salt and pepper.

8 oz./250 g. squid

Clean squid by pulling off the head and pulling out the entrails.
Lay squid on a cutting board or flat surface and using a sharp knife, scrape the skin off.
Wash squid thoroughly in cold running water.
Cut off tentacles and make sure that the beak-like mouth is discarded.
Chop tentacles and body into 1/2 inch/ 1 cm. pieces.
Pat squid dry with a cloth or paper towel.

8 oz./250 g. octopus tentacles

Wash octopus tentacles, then chop into 1/2 inch/1 cm. pieces.

Add squid and octopus tentacles to liquid and cook on medium heat for 2 minutes, stirring frequently.

8 oz./250 g. fresh clams
8 oz./250 g. fresh mussels
8 oz./250 g. fresh crab claws
8 oz./250 g. fresh prawns, shell on

Wash clams and mussels with cold running water to remove sand, then add them, and crab claws and prawns, to squid and octopus tentacles in liquid and cook on medium heat for 2 minutes, stirring frequently.

8 oz./250 g. fillet of cod,
cut into 2 inch/5 cm. squares
8 oz./250 g. fillet of red snapper,
cut into 2 inch/5 cm. squares
8 oz./250 g. fillet of salmon,
cut into 2 inch/5 cm. squares

Add cod, red snapper and salmon to squid, octopus tentacles, clams, mussels, crab claws and prawns in liquid and cook on medium heat for 7 minutes.

There should be enough liquid to cover the fish.
If there is not enough liquid to cover the fish, add wine and water in the proportion of 1:2.

salt (to taste)
freshly ground black pepper (to taste)

Season with salt and pepper.

fried bread
(see below)

Ladle cioppino over fried bread in the bottom of a soup tureen or in large soup plates and serve.

Fried Bread:

1 long loaf of French bread,
cut 2 inches/5 cm. thick
(2-3 slices per person)

oil

Coat the bottom of a skillet in oil and fry bread in oil in skillet on high heat until golden.

This recipe for Cioppino serves 6 people. Cioppino is illustrated on p. 105.

FILETTO DI POLLO AL BAROLO
Chicken Breasts in Red Wine Sauce

Pre-heat oven to 400° F/200° C.

2 whole breasts of chicken
salt (to taste)
freshly ground black pepper (to taste)
2 tbsp./30 g. flour

Bone chicken. We recommend you have your butcher do this.
Cut each chicken breast into 2 pieces.
Season chicken with salt and pepper.
Lightly flour, shaking off the excess.

1/4 cup/50 mL. olive oil

Sauté chicken on both sides in hot oil in a skillet on medium heat for 3-5 minutes per side until chicken is golden brown.

Put chicken in a shallow roasting pan and put roasting pan in oven and bake at 400° F/200° C for 15 minutes.

Sauce:

olive oil
2 shallots, finely chopped

Cover the bottom of another skillet in oil and sauté shallots in oil on medium heat until they are brown.

1 cup/250 mL. veal stock
(see p. 31)
1/2 cup/125 mL. full-bodied dry red wine (Barolo)

Add veal stock and wine to shallots, stir until well blended and reduce by simmering on medium heat until veal stock becomes velvety and sauce thickens.

2 tbsp./30 g. butter

Remove sauce from heat, add butter to shallots, veal stock and wine and stir until well blended (if veal stock is thick to begin with, use less butter; if it is too thin, use more butter).

salt (to taste)
freshly ground black pepper (to taste)

Season with salt and pepper.

Put chicken on a warm serving platter or on warm plates.
Coat with sauce and serve.

This recipe for Filetto di Pollo al Barolo serves 2 people. Filetto di Pollo al Barolo is illustrated on p. 123. The recipe for Pollo con Prosciutto e Formaggio on p. 119 serves 2 people.

POLLO CON PROSCIUTTO E FORMAGGIO
Chicken with Prosciutto and Cheese

Pre-heat oven to 350° F/180° C.

1 whole breast of chicken salt (to taste) freshly ground black pepper (to taste) 1/2 tsp./2 g. thyme 2 tsp./10 g. butter	*Bone and skin chicken. We recommend you have your butcher do this.* *Cut chicken breast into 2 pieces.* *Flatten chicken by pounding it lightly between two pieces of plastic wrap.* *Season chicken with salt and pepper.* *Sprinkle thyme on top of each chicken breast.* *Put 1 tsp./5 g. of butter in the centre of each chicken breast.*
1 oz./25 g. prosciutto, thinly sliced (2 slices)	*Put one slice of prosciutto on the inside of each chicken breast.*
1 oz./25 g. Gruyere or Emmenthal cheese, thinly sliced (2 slices)	*Put one slice of Gruyere or Emmenthal cheese on top of the prosciutto.*
	Fold chicken breast in half and secure with a toothpick.
1/4 cup/50 g. flour	*Lightly flour, shaking off the excess.*
1 tbsp./15 mL. olive oil 1 tbsp./15 g. butter	*Sauté chicken on both sides in hot oil and butter in an ovenproof skillet on medium heat until chicken is lightly browned.*
	Put skillet in oven and bake at 350° F/180° C for 15 minutes. *Remove chicken from skillet and keep warm; discard excess oil and butter from skillet.*

Sauce:

1 tbsp./15 mL. port wine 1 tbsp./15 mL. scotch whiskey	*Deglaze skillet with wine and whiskey.*
1/4 cup/50 mL. whipping cream	*Add cream to wine and whiskey, stir until well blended and reduce by simmering on medium heat until sauce thickens.*
juice of 1/4 lemon	*Squeeze lemon juice directly into wine, whiskey and cream and stir until well blended.*
salt (to taste) freshly ground black pepper (to taste)	*Season with salt and pepper.*
1/8 tsp./pinch of paprika (for colour)	*Put chicken on a warm serving platter or on warm plates.* *Coat with sauce, sprinkle with paprika and serve.*

POLLO CON ZUCCHINI FRITTI
Breast of Chicken with Sautéed Zucchini

Pre-heat oven to 350° F/180° C.

1 whole breast of chicken	*Bone chicken. We recommend you have*
salt (to taste)	*your butcher do this.*
freshly ground black pepper (to taste)	*Cut chicken breast into 2 pieces and*
2 tbsp./30 g. flour	*season with salt and pepper.*
	Lightly flour, shaking off the excess.
1 tbsp./15 mL. olive oil	*Sauté chicken, breast side down, in hot oil*
1 tbsp./15 g. butter	*and butter in a skillet on medium heat*
	for approximately 5 minutes until
	golden brown.
juice of 1/2 lemon	*Squeeze lemon juice directly onto chicken.*
1 tbsp./15 mL. dry white wine	*Add wine to skillet and brown chicken*
	on the other side on medium heat for
	approximately 5 minutes.
	Remove chicken from skillet and keep
	warm; save skillet.
	Put chicken in a casserole dish, uncovered,
	and put casserole dish in oven and bake
	at 350° F/180° C for 15 minutes.
1 medium zucchini, thinly sliced	*Season zucchini with salt and pepper.*
salt (to taste)	*Lightly flour, shaking off the excess.*
freshly ground black pepper (to taste)	
1 tbsp./15 g. flour	
1 tsp./5 mL. olive oil	*Sauté zucchini in oil and butter in another*
1 tsp./5 g. butter	*skillet on medium heat until golden brown.*
	Put zucchini on top of baked chicken.

Sauce:

2 tbsp./30 mL. port wine	*Deglaze skillet in which the chicken was*
2 tbsp./30 mL. scotch whiskey	*sautéed with wine and whiskey.*
2 tbsp./30 mL. whipping cream	*Add cream to wine and whiskey, stir until*
	well blended and reduce by simmering on
	medium heat for 3 minutes.
2 tbsp./30 mL. chicken consommé	*Add chicken consommé to wine, whiskey*
(see p. 19)	*and cream and reduce by simmering on*
	medium heat until sauce thickens.
1 tsp./5 g. fresh parsley,	*Add parsley to wine, whiskey, cream*
finely chopped	*and chicken consommé and stir until*
	well blended.

> *Put chicken on a warm serving platter*
> *or on warm plates.*
> *Coat with sauce and serve.*

This recipe for Pollo con Zucchini Fritti serves 2 people.

POLLO CONTADINA
Chicken Stewed in Tomatoes, Red Wine, Onion and Peppers

Pre-heat oven to 350° F/180° C.

1 (2 1/2 lb./1.25 kg.) whole chicken
salt (to taste)
freshly ground black pepper (to taste)
1/4 cup/50 g. flour

Cut chicken into four pieces and season
with salt and pepper.
Lightly flour, shaking off the excess.

1/4 cup/50 mL. olive oil

Sauté chicken on both sides in hot oil in a
skillet on medium heat for 3-5 minutes
per side until lightly browned.

Put chicken in a casserole dish and
set aside.

Sauce:

2 tbsp./30 g. butter
1 medium onion, sliced
2 cloves garlic, finely chopped
1 green pepper, seeded and sliced
1 red pepper, seeded and sliced

Sauté onion, garlic, green pepper and
red pepper in butter in another skillet on
medium heat for approximately 5 minutes.

1/2 cup/125 mL. dry red wine

Add wine to onion, garlic, green pepper
and red pepper and reduce by simmering
on medium heat for 2-3 minutes.

1 (28 oz./796 mL.) can
of peeled Italian tomatoes
1 bayleaf
1/8 tsp./pinch of oregano
salt (to taste)
freshly ground black pepper (to taste)

Add tomatoes, bayleaf, oregano, salt and
pepper to onion, garlic, green pepper,
red pepper and wine and stir until
well blended.

Pour sauce over chicken in casserole dish
and put casserole dish, partly covered,
in oven and bake at 350° F/180° C for
30 minutes or until chicken is cooked.

Serve from casserole dish or put on
warm plates and serve.

This recipe for Pollo Contadina serves 2 people. Pollo Contadina is illustrated on p. 123.

POLLO DIAVOLO
Grilled Chicken with Mustard Sauce

1 (2 lb./1 kg.) frying chicken
1 clove garlic, cut in slivers
1 tbsp./15 mL. olive oil
2 tsp./10 g. Dijon mustard
salt (to taste)
freshly ground black pepper (to taste)

Split chicken down the breast bone, but leave it attached by the backbone.
Flatten chicken out.
Insert slivers of garlic under the chicken skin using the edge of a sharp knife.
Rub chicken with oil and mustard.
Season with salt and pepper.
Make an incision on the inside of each thigh along the bone to allow heat to penetrate chicken and for chicken to cook faster.

2 tbsp./30 mL. olive oil

Grill chicken on both sides for 10-15 minutes per side, basting chicken with oil as it cooks and adding more oil if necessary.
To test: pierce the inside of the thigh. If the juices run clear, chicken is done. Set chicken aside and keep warm.

Mustard Sauce:

1 tbsp./15 g. butter
1 small onion, finely chopped

Sauté onion in butter in a skillet on medium heat until onion is transparent.

1 tbsp./15 mL. dry white wine
2 tbsp./30 mL. chicken consommé
(*see p. 19*)

Add wine and chicken consommé to onion and simmer on medium heat for 2-3 minutes.

juice of 1/2 lemon

Squeeze lemon juice directly into wine and chicken consommé and stir until well blended.

1 tbsp./15 g. Dijon mustard

Add mustard to onion, wine, chicken consommé and lemon juice, stir until well blended and reduce by simmering on medium heat for 2-3 minutes.

salt (to taste)
freshly ground black pepper (to taste)

Season with salt and pepper.

Put chicken on a warm serving platter or on warm plates.
Coat with sauce and serve.

This recipe for Pollo Diavolo serves 2 people.

Illustration #11: Meat, Fowl & Game. *From left to right*: Pollo Contadina, Filetto di Pollo al Barolo and Pollo Oreganato al Limone. Tiles courtesy of World Mosaic Ltd.; plates courtesy of Holt Renfrew.

POLLO OREGANATO AL LIMONE
Chicken with Oregano and Lemon

Pre-heat oven to 375° F/190° C.

1 (2 1/2 lb./1.25 kg.) whole frying chicken 2 tbsp./30 mL. olive oil	*Cut chicken in half and rub chicken* *with oil.*
salt (to taste) freshly ground black pepper (to taste) 1/8 tsp./pinch of oregano 1/8 tsp./pinch of paprika	*Season chicken with salt, pepper, oregano* *and paprika.*
	Put chicken, breast side up, in a *shallow roasting pan in oven and bake* *at 375° F/190° C for 30 minutes.*
juice of 1 lemon	*Squeeze lemon juice directly onto chicken* *in roasting pan.*
1/2 lemon, cut in wedges	*Put chicken on a warm serving platter* *or on warm plates.* *Garnish with lemon wedges and serve.*

This recipe for Pollo Oreganato al Limone serves 2 people. Pollo Oreganato al Limone is illustrated on p. 123.

Illustration #12: Meat, Fowl & Game. *At left*: Quaglie con Uva e Brandy. *At right*: Anitra con Cedro. Tiles courtesy of World Mosaic Ltd.; plates courtesy of Holt Renfrew.

POLLO ZAFFERATO
Breast of Chicken in Cream with Saffron

Pre-heat oven to 350° F/180° C.

1 whole breast of chicken
2 chicken thighs
salt (to taste)
freshly ground black pepper (to taste)
1/2 cup/125 g. flour

Bone chicken, leaving the wing bone in breast. We recommend you have your butcher do this.
Cut chicken breast into 2 pieces and season chicken with salt and pepper. Lightly flour, shaking off the excess.

1/4 cup/50 mL. olive oil

Sauté chicken breast, breast side down, and chicken thighs, in hot oil in an ovenproof skillet on medium heat for 2-3 minutes until browned.
Turn chicken over and repeat.
Leave chicken in skillet.

Sauce:

3 cups/700 mL. whipping cream
4 tsp./20 g. leek, julienned
(only the white part)
1/8 tsp./pinch of saffron

Add cream, leek and saffron to chicken in skillet and stir until well blended.

Put skillet in oven and bake at 350° F/180° C for 20-30 minutes, frequently stirring sauce so that cream does not separate.
If sauce reduces too much before chicken is cooked, add more cream.

salt (to taste)
freshly ground black pepper (to taste)

Season with salt and pepper.

1/8 tsp./pinch of paprika
(for colour)

Put chicken on a warm serving platter or on warm plates.
Stir sauce so that it is well blended and uniform in colour before serving. Coat with sauce, sprinkle with paprika and serve.

This recipe for Pollo Zafferato serves 2 people.

GALLINELLA CON FRUTTA DI STAGIONE
Cornish Game Hen Stuffed with Fruit

Pre-heat oven to 400° F/200° C.

2 (1 1/2 lb./700 g.) Cornish game hens
2 tbsp./30 g. butter, melted
salt (to taste)
freshly ground black pepper (to taste)
1 tsp./5 g. oregano

Bone game hens. We recommend you have your butcher do this.
Wash game hens inside and out.
Baste game hens with melted butter.
Pat game hens with salt and pepper and sprinkle oregano on top of hens.

Stuffing:

1 small apple, peeled and grated
1/2 cup/125 g. papaya or canteloupe, diced small
rind of 1/2 orange
2 cups/450 g. bread, cubed small
2 tbsp./30 mL. orange juice (optional)

Mix apple, papaya or canteloupe, orange rind and cubed bread together in a bowl. If mixture appears too dry or if bread is not fresh, add orange juice.

Pack the cavity of game hens with stuffing.

Put stuffed game hens in a shallow roasting pan and put roasting pan in oven and roast at 400° F/200° C for 25 minutes or until game hens are cooked. Remove game hens from roasting pan and keep warm.

Sauce:

2 tbsp./30 mL. dry white wine

Deglaze roasting pan with wine.

2 tbsp./30 mL. lemon juice

Squeeze lemon juice directly into wine and stir until well blended.

2 tsp./10 g. fresh parsley, finely chopped

Add parsley to wine and lemon juice and stir until well blended.

1/2 cup/125 mL. chicken consommé (*see p. 19*)

Add chicken consommé to wine, lemon juice and parsley, stir until well blended and reduce by simmering on medium heat until sauce thickens slightly.

2 tbsp./30 g. butter

Remove sauce from heat, add butter to wine, lemon juice, parsley and chicken consommé and stir until well blended.

orange slices
4 sprigs of fresh parsley

Put stuffed game hens on a warm serving platter or on warm plates. Coat with sauce, garnish with a twist of orange and sprigs of parsley and serve.

This recipe for Gallinella con Frutta di Stagione serves 2 people. Gallinella con Frutta di Stagione is illustrated on the cover.

FARAONA IN UMIDO
Guinea Hen with Smoked Bacon

Pre-heat oven to 350° F/180° C.

1 (2 1/2 lb./1.25 kg.) guinea hen — *Cut up guinea hen, using only the breast, thigh and leg.*

Marinade:

1/2 cup/250 mL. dry red wine
1 small onion, chopped
1 small stalk celery, chopped
2-3 sprigs of fresh parsley
and parsley stalks, chopped
1 clove garlic, chopped
1/8 tsp./pinch of thyme
1/8 tsp./pinch of oregano
a drop of lemon juice
salt (to taste)
freshly ground black pepper (to taste)
1/4 cup/50 mL. olive oil

Mix wine, onion, celery, parsley, garlic, thyme, oregano, lemon juice, salt and pepper together in a bowl or roasting pan, adding the oil last.

Submerge guinea hen in marinade by placing a plate on top of hen and marinate for 2 days, blending marinade approximately every 8 hours (the oil tends to separate).
Remove guinea hen from marinade and reserve marinade.

salt (to taste)
freshly ground black pepper (to taste) — *Season guinea hen with salt and pepper.*

1/4 cup/50 g. flour — *Lightly flour, shaking off the excess.*

2 tbsp./30 mL. olive oil — *Sauté guinea hen in hot oil in a skillet on high heat until lightly browned.*

Sauce:

Strain marinade into a saucepan through a sieve lined with a linen or muslin cloth. Save vegetables.

1 egg white — *Add egg white to marinade in saucepan and slowly bring to a boil on medium heat, skimming the froth off the top.*

1 tsp./5 mL. olive oil
1 tsp./5 g. butter — *Sauté vegetables in oil and butter in an ovenproof skillet on medium heat until vegetables are lightly browned.*

2 tbsp./30 mL. tomato paste	Add tomato paste to vegetables in skillet and stir until well blended.
	Add marinade to vegetables and tomato paste and stir until well blended.
1/2 cup/125 mL. dry red wine 2 cups/450 mL. chicken consommé (see p. 19)	Add wine and chicken consommé to vegetables, tomato paste and marinade and stir until well blended.
	Add guinea hen to vegetables, tomato paste, marinade, wine and chicken consommé and put skillet in oven and braise at 350° F/180° C for 45 minutes.
	Remove guinea hen from skillet and bone breast (see p. 132); keep guinea hen warm. Coarsely chop guinea hen bones and add them to the sauce. Reduce sauce by simmering on medium heat for 15-20 minutes, then strain into a saucepan through a sieve lined with a linen or muslin cloth, separating the bones from the sauce. Return sauce to medium heat and slowly bring to a boil, skimming the froth off the top. Reduce sauce by simmering on medium heat until it is thick enough to coat the back of a spoon.
2 tbsp./30 g. butter	Remove sauce from heat, add butter to sauce and stir until well blended.

Smoked Bacon:

3-4 oz./85-125 g. smoked bacon, lard on (3-4 slices), cut to 1 x 1 1/4 inches/2.5 x 3 cm.	Fry bacon in a skillet on medium heat until golden brown.
2-3 mushrooms, sliced 6-8 pearl onions	Add mushrooms and onions to bacon and sauté on medium heat for 1-2 minutes; discard excess fat from skillet.
2 tsp./10 g. fresh parsley, finely chopped	Put guinea hen on a warm serving platter or on warm plates. Coat with sauce, garnish with smoked bacon, mushrooms and onions, sprinkle with parsley and serve.

This recipe for Faraona in Umido serves 2 people.

QUAGLIE CON UVA E BRANDY
Quail with Grape and Brandy Sauce

Pre-heat oven to 400° F/200° C.

4-6 (2 oz./50 g.) quail
salt (to taste)
freshly ground black pepper (to taste)

Bone quail, leaving in the wing bone and the leg bone (see p. 132).
Lightly season quail with salt and peper.

Stuffing:

1/4 cup/50 g. day-old white bread, cubed
1 tsp./5 g. onion, finely chopped
1 tbsp./15 g. celery, finely chopped
1 small clove garlic, finely chopped
1/8 tsp./pinch of oregano
1 egg

Mix cubed bread, onion, celery, garlic, oregano and egg together in a bowl.

Put 1 tbsp./15 g. of stuffing in each quail and close bird by bringing sides together and overlapping skin at top, then secure by weaving wooden cocktail sticks through skin.

1/4 cup/50 mL. vegetable oil

Sear stuffed quail on both sides in hot oil in an ovenproof skillet on high heat until browned.

Put skillet in oven and bake at 400° F/200° C for 5-8 minutes (quail meat is slightly red even when thoroughly cooked).
Remove quail from skillet and keep warm; discard excess oil from skillet.

Grape and Brandy Sauce:

1/4 cup/50 mL. brandy

Deglaze skillet with brandy.

12-15 green or purple grapes, halved, seeded and skinned

Add grapes to brandy and sauté on medium heat for 1-2 minutes.

1/4 cup/50 mL. veal stock
(see p. 31)

Add veal stock to brandy and grapes, stir until well blended and reduce by simmering on medium heat until sauce is thick enough to coat the back of a spoon.

salt (to taste)
freshly ground black pepper (to taste)

Season with salt and pepper.

Put quail on a warm serving platter or on warm plates.
Coat with sauce and serve.

This recipe for Quaglie con Uva e Brandy serves 2 people. Quaglie con Uva e Brandy is illustrated on p. 124.

PERNICE RIPIENA ARROSTITA
Partridge Stuffed with Wild Rice

Pre-heat oven to 350° F/180° C.

2 (1 lb./450 g.) partridges
salt (to taste)
freshly ground black pepper (to taste)
1/4 tsp./1 g. oregano

*Bone partridges, leaving in the wing bone
and the leg bone (see p. 132).
Pat partridges with salt and pepper.
Sprinkle oregano on top of partridges.*

Stuffing:

1 cup/250 g. cooked wild rice
1 oz./25 g. pâté de foie gras,
chopped (available in tins)
2-3 mushrooms, sliced
2 tbsp./30 g. fresh parsley,
finely chopped
1 small shallot, finely chopped
1 tbsp./15 g. butter
2 tbsp./30 mL. brandy
2 tbsp./30 mL. white sauce
(see p. 32)

*Mix wild rice, pâté de foie gras,
mushrooms, parsley, shallot, butter,
brandy and white sauce together in a
bowl.*

*Put 1/2 cup/125 g. of stuffing in each
partridge and close bird by bringing sides
together and overlapping skin at top, then
pull neck skin over seam and secure by
weaving wooden cocktail sticks
through skin.*

butter

*Put stuffed partridges, breast side up, in a
buttered baking pan and put baking pan
in oven and roast at 350° F/180° C for
20-25 minutes.
Remove stuffed partridge from pan
and keep warm.*

Sauce:

2 tbsp./30 mL. grappa
2 tbsp./30 mL. dry white wine

*Deglaze baking pan with grappa and
wine.*

1/4 cup/50 mL. veal stock
(see p. 31)

*Add veal stock to grappa and wine and
reduce by simmering on medium heat
until sauce is thick enough to coat the
back of a spoon.*

1 tsp./5 g. butter

*Remove sauce from heat, add butter to
grappa, wine and veal stock and stir
until well blended.*

(cont'd over)

Cont'd from page 131

salt (to taste)
freshly ground black pepper (to taste)

Season with salt and pepper.

Put partridges on a warm serving platter or on warm plates.
Coat with sauce and serve.

This recipe for Pernice Ripiena Arrostita serves 2 people.

Boning:

When serving small game birds that are to be stuffed, they are preferably cooked and served with the breast and back bones removed to make for easier eating. To remove these bones, first chill the bird for 1 hour until the flesh is firm, then with a sharp boning knife or similar knife, make an incision along the back of the bird from the neck to the tail, and following closely to the bone, begin to cut down, slowly working the flesh free from the carcass until the leg and wing joints have been reached. These should be separated by bending the joint back and then severing it from the body, taking care not to pierce the skin. Continue until the breast and back bones have all been removed. Fill the bird with its appropriate stuffing and seal with either a wooden skewer or wooden cocktail stick.

ANITRA ALL' ARANCIO
Duck with Orange Sauce

Pre-heat oven to 450° F/230° C.

1 (3 lb./1.5 kg.) duck
salt (to taste)
freshly ground black pepper (to taste)

Remove giblets and neck from cavity of duck and cut off wing tips at joints.
Wash duck inside and out.
Pat duck with salt and pepper.

Duck Stock:

1 tsp./5 mL. olive oil
2 tsp./10 g. butter
1 small onion, diced large
1 small carrot, diced large
1 stalk celery and celery top,
diced large

Chop giblets, neck and wing tips from duck and sauté with onion, carrot and celery in oil and butter in a casserole dish on high heat for approximately 5 minutes until meat is browned.

Put casserole dish in oven and bake at 450° F/230° C for 15 minutes.

1/4 cup/50 mL. dry white wine

Deglaze casserole dish with wine, then empty ingredients into a saucepan.

3 cups/700 mL. cold water

Cover ingredients with water and bring to a boil on high heat, then reduce by two-thirds by simmering on low heat.

Strain stock into another saucepan through a sieve lined with a linen or muslin cloth and return to medium heat. Discard giblets, neck, wing tips and vegetables.

1 1/2 tbsp./20 g. butter
1 tbsp./15 g. flour

Mix butter and flour together in a skillet on medium heat, stirring constantly, to make a roux, then add roux, bit by bit, to duck stock in saucepan, stir until well blended and simmer on medium heat for at least 5 minutes.

Put duck in shallow roasting pan and put roasting pan in oven and roast at 450° F/230° C for approximately 1 hour (15-20 minutes per pound/30-40 minutes per kilogram).
Turn oven off and leave duck in oven for another 10 minutes — this prevents the skin from burning and allows the inner meat to continue cooking.

(cont'd over)

Cont'd from page 133

Orange Sauce (takes 10 minutes):

1 tsp./5 g. butter 2 tsp./10 g. brown sugar	*Melt butter in a skillet on medium heat, then add sugar and stir until well blended.*
1/4 cup/50 mL. orange juice, freshly squeezed 1 cup/250 mL. duck stock (see p. 133) 2 tbsp./30 mL. Grand Marnier or any sweet orange liqueur rind of 1/2 orange	*Add orange juice, duck stock, Grand Marnier and orange rind to butter and sugar, stir until well blended and reduce by simmering on medium heat until sauce is thick enough to coat duck.*
salt (to taste) freshly ground black pepper (to taste)	*Season with salt and pepper.*
1/2 orange, cut into slices 6-8 sprigs of watercress	*Put duck on a warm serving platter and carve into slices.* *Put duck slices on warm plates.* *Coat with sauce, garnish with orange slices and watercress and serve.*

This recipe for Anitra all' Arancio serves 2 people.

ANITRA CON CEDRO
Duck with Honey and Lime Sauce

Pre-heat oven to 450° F/230° C.

1 (3 lb./1.5 kg.) duck
salt (to taste)
freshly ground black pepper (to taste)

Remove giblets and neck from cavity of duck and cut off wing tips at joints. Wash duck inside and out. Pat duck with salt and pepper.

1 tbsp./15 mL. honey
juice of 1/2 lime
2 tbsp./30 mL. dry white wine

Mix honey, lime juice and wine together in a saucepan and warm on medium heat.

Lightly baste duck once with honey, lime juice and wine mixture, reserving some for the sauce.

Put duck in a shallow roasting pan and put roasting pan in oven and roast at 450° F/230° C for approximately 1 hour (15-20 minutes per pound/30-40 minutes per kilogram).
Turn oven off and leave duck in oven for another 10 minutes — this prevents the skin from burning and allows the inner meat to continue cooking.

Honey and Lime Sauce:

1 cup/250 mL. duck stock
(see p. 133)

Add duck stock to remaining honey, lime juice and wine mixture, stir until well blended and reduce by simmering on medium heat until sauce is thick enough to coat duck.

salt (to taste)
freshly ground black pepper (to taste)

Season with salt and pepper.

1 lime, cut into slices
(without the rind)

Put duck on a warm serving platter and carve into slices. Put duck slices on warm plates. Coat with sauce, garnish with rindless lime slices and serve.

This recipe for Anitra con Cedro serves 2 people. Anitra con Cedro is illustrated on p. 124.

FAGIANO CON FUNGHI E CHAMPAGNE
Pheasant with Mushroom and Champagne Sauce

Pre-heat oven to 500° F/240° C.

1 (2 1/2-3 lb./1.25-1.5 kg.) pheasant
oil
salt (to taste)
freshly ground black pepper (to taste)
1 head of garlic, halved

Remove giblets and neck from cavity of pheasant and cut off wing tips at joints.
Wash pheasant inside and out.
Brush pheasant with oil.
Pat pheasant with salt and pepper.
Put garlic, sliced in half, in cavity of pheasant.

Pheasant Stock:

1 tsp./5 mL. olive oil
2 tsp./10 g. butter
1 small onion, diced large
1 small carrot, diced large
1 stalk of celery and celery top, diced large

Chop giblets, neck and wing tips from pheasant and sauté with onion, carrot and celery in oil and butter in a casserole dish on high heat for approximately 5 minutes until meat is browned.

Put casserole dish in oven and bake at 500° F/240° C for 15 minutes.

1/4 cup/50 mL. dry white wine

Deglaze casserole dish with wine, then empty ingredients into a saucepan.

2 cups/450 mL. cold water

Cover ingredients with water and bring to a boil on high heat, then reduce by two-thirds by simmering on medium heat.

Strain stock into another saucepan through a sieve lined with a linen or muslin cloth and return to medium heat.

1 1/2 tbsp./20 g. butter
1 tbsp./15 g. flour

Mix butter and flour together in a skillet on medium heat, stirring constantly, to make a roux, then add roux, bit by bit, to pheasant stock in saucepan, stir until well blended and simmer on medium heat for at least 5 minutes.

Put pheasant in a shallow roasting pan and put roasting pan in oven and roast at a reduced heat of 425° F/220° C for 35-40 minutes.

Mushroom and Champagne Sauce:

1 tsp./5 g. butter
8 large mushroom caps, thinly sliced
1 tsp./5 g. shallot or onion, finely chopped

Sauté mushroom caps and shallot or onion in butter in a skillet on medium heat until mushrooms are light brown; discard excess butter from skillet.

1/3 cup/75 mL. champagne or sparkling white wine	*Add champagne or sparkling white wine to mushroom caps and shallot or onion and simmer until one-half the champagne has evaporated.*
3/4 cup/175 mL. pheasant stock (*see p. 136*)	*Add pheasant stock to mushroom caps, shallot or onion and champagne or sparkling white wine and reduce by simmering until sauce thickens.*
2 tbsp./30 mL. whipping cream 1 tsp./5 mL. lemon juice	*Add cream and lemon juice to mushroom caps, shallot or onion, champagne or sparkling white wine and pheasant stock and stir until well blended.*
1/4 cup/50 g. butter	*Remove sauce from heat, add butter to mushroom caps, shallot or onion, champagne or sparkling white wine, pheasant stock, cream and lemon juice and stir until well blended.*
salt (to taste) freshly ground black pepper (to taste)	*Season with salt and pepper.*
2 sprigs of fresh parsley	*Put pheasant on a warm serving platter and carve into slices.* *Put pheasant slices on warm plates.* *Coat with sauce, garnish with sprigs of parsley and serve.*

This recipe for Fagiano con Funghi e Champagne serves 2 people.

TACCHINO RIPIENO CON SALSICCE E CASTAGNE
Turkey Stuffed with Sausage and Chestnut

Pre-heat oven to 450° F/230° C.

1 (15 lb./7.5 kg.) turkey salt (to taste) freshly ground black pepper (to taste)	*Remove giblets and neck from cavity of turkey and set aside.* *Wash turkey inside and out.* *Season turkey well with salt and pepper.*

Turkey Stock:

4 cups/900 mL. cold water	*Put turkey giblets and neck in a pot and cover them with water.* *Bring water to a boil on high heat, then reduce by one-quarter by simmering on low heat for 1 hour, frequently skimming the froth off the top.* *Strain stock into a bowl through a sieve lined with a linen or muslin cloth and set aside.* *Discard giblets and neck.*

Stuffing (while stock is simmering):

1 lb./450 g. fresh chestnuts cold water	*Put chestnuts in a pot and cover them with water.* *Bring water to a boil on high heat and cook chestnuts on high heat for 2-3 minutes.* *Remove pot from heat and allow chestnuts to cool, then peel.* *Put chestnuts back in pot and simmer on medium heat for approximately 45 minutes or until tender.* *Chop chestnuts coarsely and set aside.*
3 tbsp./45 g. butter 1 large onion, finely chopped	*Sauté onion in butter in a skillet on medium heat until onion is transparent.*
2 stalks celery, finely chopped	*Add celery to onion and sauté on medium heat for 1 minute.*
1 lb./450 g. sausage, diced small	*Add sausage to onion and celery and sauté on medium heat for 4-5 minutes.* *Put onion, celery and sausage in a bowl and mix together.*
2 sprigs of fresh parsley, finely chopped 1 tsp./5 g. thyme, finely chopped salt (to taste) freshly ground black pepper (to taste)	*Season with parsley, thyme, salt and pepper.*

4 cups/900 g. bread, cubed 1 cup/250 mL. milk	Put bread in another bowl and saturate bread with milk, then using your hands, squeeze excess milk from bread.
	Add bread to onion, celery and sausage and mix together; discard excess milk.
1/4 cup/50 mL. brandy	Add chopped chestnuts and brandy to onion, celery, sausage and bread and mix together thoroughly.
	Loosely fill the cavity and crop of turkey with stuffing.
	Sew cavity and crop of turkey shut or skewer shut with wooden cocktail sticks.
3 tbsp./45 g. butter	Rub turkey skin with butter.
1 large onion, sliced 1 carrot, diced large 2 stalks celery and celery tops, diced large	Put turkey, breast side down, in a roasting pan and surround it with vegetables.
2 cups/450 mL. cold water	Pour water into roasting pan.
	Put roasting pan in oven and roast at 450° F/230° C for 10 minutes.
	Turn turkey over, breast side up, and roast at 450° F/230° C for another 10 minutes.
	Cover turkey with brown paper that has been brushed with butter or oil, reduce heat to 325° F/160° C and roast for 3 hours (12 minutes per pound/25 minutes per kilogram), frequently lifting the brown paper and basting the turkey. Remove brown paper 45 minutes before turkey is done so that the turkey skin will brown. Remove turkey from roasting pan and keep warm; skim excess fat from roasting pan and put roasting pan on high heat on stove.

Sauce:

1-2 tbsp./15-30 g. flour	Sprinkle flour in roasting pan and using a wooden spoon, scrape sides and bottom of pan, stirring in turkey juices, vegetables and any bits of turkey left there.
3 cups/700 mL. turkey stock (see p. 138)	Add turkey stock to roasting pan, stir until well blended with flour and simmer on medium heat for 5 minutes.

(cont'd over)

Cont'd from page 139

	Strain sauce into a saucepan through a sieve lined with a linen or muslin cloth. Discard vegetables caught in linen or muslin cloth. Return sauce to stove and simmer on low heat for 10 minutes.
salt (to taste) freshly ground black pepper (to taste)	*Season with salt and pepper.*
	Pour sauce into a sauceboat.
	Put turkey on a warm serving platter and carve into slices. Put turkey slices on warm plates. Serve with sauce on the side.

This recipe for Tacchino Ripieno con Salsicce e Castagne serves 12 people.

INVOLTINI DI TACCHINO
Turkey with Belgian Endive Pizzaiola

Pre-heat oven to 400° F/200° C.

2 (6-8 oz./175-250 g.) fillets of turkey
salt (to taste)
freshly ground black pepper (to taste)
1 tsp./5 g. shallot, finely chopped
or 1 tsp./5 g. garlic, finely chopped
1/4 tsp./1 g. oregano

Pound turkey lightly to flatten it.
Season turkey with salt and pepper.
Season one side of turkey fillet with shallot or garlic and oregano.

1 cup/250 mL. chicken consommé
(*see p. 19*)
2 tbsp./30 mL. dry white wine or water

Put chicken consommé and wine or water in a saucepan and bring to a boil on high heat.

2 leaves of medium Belgian endive

Add endive to chicken consommé and wine or water and boil for 1 minute, then drain.

Put endive on the side of the turkey fillet seasoned with shallot or garlic and oregano, roll up and secure with a wooden cocktail stick.

1 tbsp./15 g. flour

Lightly dust turkey fillets with flour.

1/4 cup/50 mL. olive oil
or vegetable oil

Sauté turkey fillets on both sides in hot oil in an ovenproof skillet on high heat until lightly browned; discard excess oil from skillet and remove wooden cocktail sticks from turkey fillets.

1 cup/250 mL. tomato sauce
(*see p. 33*)

Pour tomato sauce over turkey fillets.

2 tbsp./30 mL. dry white wine

Add wine to tomato sauce and stir until well blended.

1 oz./25 g. Mozzarella cheese,
sliced medium (2 slices)

Put Mozzarella cheese slices on top of turkey fillets and tomato sauce.

Put skillet in oven and bake at 400° F/200° C for 12-15 minutes.

2 tsp./10 g. fresh parsley,
finely chopped

Put turkey fillets on a warm serving platter or on warm plates.
Garnish with parsley and serve.

This recipe for Involtini di Tacchino serves 2 people.

OCA FARCITA BONGUSTAIO
Roast Stuffed Goose

Pre-heat oven to 450° F/230° C.

1 (8-9 lb./4-4.5 kg.) goose salt (to taste) freshly ground black pepper (to taste)	*Remove giblets and neck from cavity of goose and set goose liver aside.* *Wash goose inside and out.* *Pat goose with lots of salt and a lesser amount of pepper.*

Goose Stock:

1 tbsp./15 g. butter 1 onion, chopped 1 carrot, chopped 1 stalk celery and celery top, chopped	*Chop giblets and neck from goose and sauté with onion, carrot and celery in butter in a casserole dish on high heat for approximately 5 minutes until meat is browned.*

Put casserole dish in oven and bake at 450° F/230° C for 15 minutes.

Empty ingredients into a saucepan.

1 quart/1 L. cold water	*Cover ingredients with water and bring to a boil on high heat, then reduce by two-thirds by simmering on medium heat.*

Strain stock into another saucepan through a sieve lined with a linen or muslin cloth and return to medium heat.

1 1/2 tbsp./20 g. butter 1 tbsp./15 g. flour	*Mix butter and flour together in a skillet on medium heat, stirring constantly, to make a roux, then add roux, bit by bit, to goose stock in saucepan, stir until well blended and simmer on medium heat for at least 5 minutes.*

Stuffing:

2 tbsp./30 g. butter 1 onion, chopped goose liver, chopped	*Sauté onion and goose liver in butter in a skillet on medium heat for 2-3 minutes.*
1 apple, peeled, cored and finely chopped 1 tbsp./15 g. sage 1 tsp./5 g. fresh parsley, finely chopped 3 cups/700 g. bread, cubed	*Mix apple, sage, parsley and cubed bread together in a bowl.*

Fold apple, sage, parsley and cubed bread into onion and goose liver and mix together.

salt (to taste) freshly ground black pepper (to taste)	*Season with salt and pepper.*
	Pack cavity of goose with stuffing.
	Sew cavity of goose shut or skewer shut with a metal skewer.
1 onion, chopped 1 carrot, chopped 1 stalk celery and celery top, chopped	*Put goose in a shallow roasting pan and surround it with onion, carrot and celery.*
1 cup/250 mL. cold water	*Pour water into roasting pan.*
	Put roasting pan in oven and roast at 450° F/230° C for 15 minutes, then reduce heat to 325° F/160° C and roast for 2 hours (15 minutes per pound/ 30 minutes per kilogram). *Remove goose from roasting pan and keep warm; discard excess fat from roasting pan and put roasting pan on high heat on stove.*

Sauce:

1/4 cup/50 mL. port wine	*Deglaze roasting pan with wine.*
1 1/2 cups/350 mL. goose stock (see p. 142)	*Add goose stock to wine, stir until well blended and reduce by simmering on medium heat until sauce is thick enough to coat goose.*
	Put goose on a warm serving platter and carve into slices. *Put goose slices on warm plates.* *Coat with sauce and serve.*

This recipe for Oca Farcita Bongustaio serves 4-6 people.

CONIGLIO ARROSTO
Roast Rabbit

Pre-heat oven to 400° F/200° C.

1 (3 lb./1.5 kg.) rabbit	Season rabbit heavily with salt and
salt (to taste)	pepper.
freshly ground black pepper (to taste)	Rub rabbit with mustard.
1 tbsp./15 g. Dijon mustard	Sprinkle thyme on top of rabbit and using
1/2 tsp./2 g. thyme	the edge of a sharp knife, insert slivers of
1 clove garlic, cut in slivers	garlic into the surface of the rabbit.

2 tbsp./30 mL. olive oil — Sear both sides of rabbit in hot oil and
2 tbsp./30 g. butter — butter in a skillet on high heat for
a total of 2-3 minutes.

olive oil — Coat the bottom of a roasting pan with
oil and put rabbit in roasting pan.

Put roasting pan in oven and roast at
400° F/200° C for 35 minutes.

Put rabbit on a warm serving platter.
Carve rabbit and serve.

FILETTO DI CAPRIOLO PEPATO
Reindeer Steak with Pepper and Brandy Sauce

4 (3 oz./85 g.) fillets of reindeer, — Season reindeer with salt and
cut from the leg or loin — press crushed peppercorns into reindeer
salt (to taste) — so that they adhere to the meat.
1 tsp./5 g. peppercorns, crushed

olive oil — Cover the bottom of a heavy cast iron
skillet in oil and sear reindeer in hot oil
on high heat for 1 minute per side
(longer for well-done).
Remove reindeer from skillet and keep
warm.

Pepper and Brandy Sauce:

1/4 cup/50 mL. brandy — Deglaze skillet with brandy.

1/3 cup/75 mL. whipping cream — Add cream and crushed peppercorns to
1/2 tsp./2 g. peppercorns, crushed — brandy and reduce by simmering on
medium heat for 2-3 minutes.

2 sprigs of watercress — Put reindeer on a warm serving platter
or on warm plates.
Coat with sauce, garnish with sprigs of
watercress and serve.

ANIMELLE DI VITELLO
Sweetbreads

12 oz./350 g. calf sweetbreads cold water 1 tsp./5 g. salt	*Cover sweetbreads with cold water in a saucepan and add salt.* *Soak sweetbreads for 3-4 hours, changing the water at least once, then drain.*
1 tsp./5 mL. vinegar or juice of 1/2 lemon	*Add vinegar or lemon juice to water in saucepan and bring to a boil on high heat. Add sweetbreads and cook just below the boiling point for approximately 3 minutes until they turn white.* *Drain and rinse with cold running water. Peel membrane and remove any gristle from sweetbreads, then slice 1/2 inch/1 cm. thick.*
salt (to taste) freshly ground black pepper (to taste)	*Season with salt and pepper.*
1/4 cup/50 g. flour	*Lightly flour, shaking off the excess.*
2 tbsp./30 g. butter	*Sauté sweetbreads in butter in a large skillet on medium heat for 2-3 minutes, turning sweetbreads over and browning both sides.* *Leave sweetbreads in skillet.*

Sauce:

1/4 cup/50 mL. veal stock (see p. 31) 1/4 cup/50 mL. dry white wine juice of 1/2 lemon 1/2 tbsp./7 g. fresh parsley, finely chopped 1 tbsp./15 g. capers, drained	*Add veal stock, wine, lemon juice, parsley and capers to sweetbreads in skillet, stir until well blended and reduce by simmering on medium heat for approximately 10 minutes, frequently turning sweetbreads over.*
salt (to taste) freshly ground black pepper (to taste)	*Season with salt and pepper.*
	Put sweetbreads on a warm serving platter or on warm plates. *Coat with sauce and serve.*

This recipe for Animelle di Vitello serves 2 people. The recipe for Coniglio Arrosto on p. 144 serves 4 people. Serve with a hot or cold Salsa Aioli (see p. 32). The recipe for Filetto di Capriolo Repato on p. 144 serves 2 people.

MEDAGLIONI DI VITELLO BOSCAIOLO
Medallions of Veal in Mushroom Sauce

4 (4 oz./125 g.) fillets of veal, cut into medallions 1 1/2 inches/4 cm. thick
salt (to taste)
freshly ground black pepper (to taste)
1 tsp./5 g. Dijon mustard

Season veal with salt and pepper.
Rub veal with mustard.

1 tbsp./15 mL. olive oil
1 tbsp./15 g. butter

Sauté veal on both sides in hot oil and butter in a skillet on medium heat for 2 minutes per side until golden brown. Remove veal from skillet and keep warm.

Mushroom Sauce:

1 tsp./5 mL. olive oil
1 tsp./5 g. butter
1/4 cup/50 g. mushrooms, sliced

Sauté mushrooms in oil and butter in skillet on medium heat for approximately 3 minutes until brown.

1 clove garlic, finely chopped

Add garlic to mushrooms and sauté on medium heat for approximately 1 minute, careful not to burn the garlic.

2 tbsp./30 mL. dry white wine

Add wine to mushrooms and garlic and simmer on medium heat for 1-2 minutes.

3/4 cup/175 mL. whipping cream

Add cream to mushrooms, garlic and wine, stir until well blended and reduce by simmering on medium heat for approximately 4 minutes until sauce thickens slightly.

salt (to taste)
freshly ground black pepper (to taste)

Season with salt and pepper.

2 tsp./10 g. fresh parsley, finely chopped

Put veal on a warm serving platter or on warm plates.
Coat with sauce, sprinkle with parsley and serve.

This recipe for Medaglioni di Vitello Boscaiolo serves 2 people.

NODINO DI VITELLO ALL' AGLIO
Fillet of Veal with Garlic Sauce

Pre-heat oven to 350° F/180° C.

2 (8 oz./250 g.) fillets of veal
salt (to taste)
freshly ground black pepper (to taste)
2 tbsp./30 g. Dijon mustard

Season veal with salt and pepper.
Rub veal with mustard.

1 tbsp./15 mL. olive oil
1 tbsp./15 g. butter

Sauté veal on both sides in hot oil
and butter in an ovenproof skillet or
casserole dish on medium heat for
2 minutes per side until golden brown.

Put skillet or casserole dish, uncovered,
in oven and bake at 350° F/180° C
for 10 minutes.
Remove veal from skillet or casserole dish
and keep warm; discard oil and butter
from skillet.

Garlic Sauce:

1 tbsp./15 mL. olive oil
1 tsp./5 g. butter
1 clove garlic, finely chopped

Sauté garlic in oil and butter in skillet or
casserole dish on medium heat for
approximately 1 minute, careful
not to burn the garlic.

2 tbsp./30 mL. dry white wine
2 tbsp./30 mL. veal stock
(see p. 31)

Deglaze skillet or casserole dish with
wine and veal stock.

1 tsp./5 g. fresh parsley,
finely chopped

Add parsley to garlic, wine and veal
stock and stir until well blended.

1/4 cup/50 mL. whipping cream

Add cream to garlic, wine, veal stock
and parsley and reduce by one-half
by simmering on medium heat for
3-4 minutes, stirring constantly.

salt (to taste)
freshly ground black pepper (to taste)

Season with salt and pepper.

1-2 watercress or sorrel leaves

Put veal on a warm serving platter
or on warm plates.
Coat with sauce, garnish with watercress
or sorrel leaves and serve.

This recipe for Nodino di Vitello all' Aglio serves 2 people.

SCALOPPINE AL LIMONE
Veal Scallops in Lemon Sauce

1 (10 oz./300 g.) veal loin, cut into scallops 1/2 inch/1 cm. thick
salt (to taste)
freshly ground black pepper (to taste)
2 tbsp./30 g. flour

Pound veal lightly to flatten it.
Season veal with salt and pepper.
Lightly flour, shaking off the excess.

. 1 tsp./5 mL. olive oil
1 tsp./5 g. butter

Sauté veal on both sides in hot oil and butter in a skillet on medium heat for 2 minutes per side until golden brown. Leave veal in skillet.

Lemon Sauce:

2 tbsp./30 mL. dry white wine

Deglaze skillet with wine.

juice of 1/2 lemon

Squeeze lemon juice directly onto veal and into wine and stir until well blended.

1 tbsp./15 g. butter
1 tsp./5 g. fresh parsley, finely chopped

Add butter and parsley to veal, wine and lemon juice, stir until well blended and reduce sauce by simmering on medium heat for approximately 4 minutes.

1/2 lemon, cut in wedges

Put veal on a warm serving platter or on warm plates.
Coat with sauce, garnish with lemon wedges and serve.

This recipe for Scaloppine al Limone serves 2 people.

SCALOPPINE AL MARSALA
Veal Scallops in Marsala Wine

1 (10 oz./300 g.) veal loin, cut into scallops 1/2 inch/1 cm. thick
salt (to taste)
freshly ground black pepper (to taste)
2 tbsp./30 g. flour

Pound veal lightly to flatten it.
Season veal with salt and pepper.
Lightly flour, shaking off the excess.

1 tsp./5 mL. olive oil
1 tsp./5 g. butter

Sauté veal on both sides in hot oil and butter in a skillet on medium heat for 2 minutes per side until golden brown. Remove veal from skillet and keep warm.

Sauce:

1/2 cup/125 mL. dry Marsala wine

Deglaze skillet with wine.

1/2 cup/125 mL. veal stock (see p. 31)

Add veal stock to wine, stir until well blended and reduce by one-third by simmering on medium heat for 2-3 minutes.

1 tbsp./15 g. butter

Remove wine and veal stock from heat, add butter and stir until well blended.

salt (to taste)
freshly ground black pepper (to taste)

Season with salt and pepper.

Put veal on a warm serving platter or on warm plates.
Coat with sauce and serve.

This recipe for Scaloppine al Marsala serves 2 people.

SCALOPPINE ALLA NAPOLETANA
Veal Scallops with Eggplant and Tomatoes

Pre-heat oven to 350° F/180° C.

1 (10 oz./300 g.) veal loin,
cut into scallops 1/2 inch/1 cm. thick
salt (to taste)
freshly ground black pepper (to taste)
1/4 cup/50 g. flour

Pound veal until it is very thin.
Season veal with salt and pepper.
Lightly flour, shaking off the excess.

1 tsp./5 mL. olive oil
1 tsp./5 g. butter

Sauté veal on both sides in hot oil and
butter in a skillet on medium heat for
2 minutes per side until golden brown.

1 small eggplant
1/4 cup/50 g. flour

Slice eggplant 1/4 inch/.5 cm. thick.
Lightly flour only 4 slices of eggplant,
shaking off the excess.

vegetable oil

Cover the bottom of a skillet in oil to a
depth of 1/4 inch/.5 cm. and fry eggplant
on both sides in hot oil on high heat
until golden and crispy.
Drain eggplant on a cloth or paper towel.

butter

Butter the bottom of a casserole dish and
put slices of eggplant on bottom of the
casserole dish.

Put veal on top of eggplant.

Sauce:

1/4 cup/50 mL. white sauce
(see p. 32)

Coat veal with white sauce.

1/2 cup/125 mL. tomato sauce
(see p. 33)

Cover white sauce with tomato sauce.

2 tbsp./30 g. Parmesan cheese,
coarsely grated
1/8 tsp./pinch of fresh oregano

Sprinkle Parmesan cheese and oregano
on top of veal, eggplant, white sauce
and tomato sauce.

Put casserole dish, uncovered, in oven
and bake at 350° F/180° C for
20 minutes.

Put veal and eggplant on a warm serving
platter or on warm plates.
Coat with sauce and serve.

This recipe for Scaloppine alla Napoletana serves 2 people.

SCALOPPINE DI VITELLO INPANATE
Breaded Veal Scallops

1 (12 oz./350 g.) veal loin, cut into scallops 1/2 inch/1 cm. thick	*Pound veal until it is very thin.*
salt (to taste)	*Season veal with salt and pepper.*
freshly ground black pepper (to taste)	*Lightly flour, shaking off the excess.*
1/4 cup/50 g. flour	
2 eggs	*Beat eggs in a bowl, then dip veal in eggs.*
1 cup/250 g. bread crumbs	*Put bread crumbs in another bowl and dip veal in bread crumbs.*
1 tbsp./15 mL. olive oil 1 tbsp./15 g. butter	*Sauté veal on both sides in hot oil and butter in a skillet on medium heat for 2-3 minutes per side until bread crumbs are golden brown.*
	Remove veal from skillet and pat dry with a cloth or paper towel to absorb the excess oil and butter.
2 tbsp./30 g. Parmesan cheese, coarsely grated	*Put veal in a casserole dish and sprinkle with Parmesan cheese.*
	Put casserole dish in oven and broil until cheese melts.

Lemon Butter (while veal is under broiler):

1/4 cup/50 g. butter	*Melt butter in a skillet on medium heat until it turns golden brown.*
juice of 1/2 lemon	*Squeeze lemon juice directly into butter and stir until well blended.*
1/2 lemon, cut in wedges	*Put veal on a warm serving platter or on warm plates.*
	Coat with sauce, garnish with lemon wedges and serve.

This recipe for Scaloppine di Vitello Inpanate serves 2 people.

SCALOPPINE MARINARA
Prawns Rolled in Scallops of Veal

1 (8 oz./250 g.) veal loin, cut into scallops 1/2 inch/1 cm. thick	*Pound veal lightly and make 6 veal scallops approximately 5 x 4 inches/ 12.5 x 10 cm. in size — to go with prawns.*
1 tsp./5 g. butter 1 tbsp./15 g. gremolata (*see p. 161*)	*Spread a small amount of butter and a small amount of gremolata on each veal scallop.*
6 large prawns, peeled and cleaned 1 tbsp./15 mL. olive oil 1 tbsp./15 g. butter	*Sauté prawns in hot oil and butter in a skillet on medium heat for 3-4 minutes.*
1/4 cup/50 mL. dry white wine	*Add wine to prawns and reduce by simmering on medium heat for approximately 1 minute.*
	Put one prawn in the centre of each veal scallop and roll up, then skewer with a toothpick.
	This part of the recipe can be made ahead.
salt (to taste)	*Season veal and prawns with salt.*
1/2 cup/125 g. flour	*Lightly flour, shaking off the excess.*
1 tbsp./15 mL. olive oil 1 tsp./5 g. butter	*Sauté veal and prawns on all sides in hot oil and butter in a skillet on medium heat for 2 minutes until golden brown. Leave veal and prawns in skillet.*

Sauce:

1/4 cup/50 mL. dry white wine	*Deglaze skillet with wine.*
3/4 cup/175 mL. whipping cream	*Add cream to veal and prawns and wine, stir until well blended and reduce by simmering on medium heat for approximately 4 minutes until sauce thickens slightly.*
2 tsp./10 g. fresh parsley, finely chopped 1/8 tsp./pinch of paprika (for colour)	*Put veal and prawns on a warm serving platter or on warm plates. Coat with sauce, sprinkle with parsley and paprika and serve.*

This recipe for Scaloppine Marinara serves 2 people.

VITELLO UMBERTO DI SAVOIA
Fillet of Veal Topped with Mozzarella Cheese

Pre-heat oven to 400° F/200° C.

1 (12 oz./350 g.) fillet of veal, cut into medallions 1 1/2 inches/4 cm. thick
salt (to taste)
freshly ground black pepper (to taste)
2 tbsp./30 g. flour

Pound veal until it is very thin.
Season veal with salt and pepper.
Lightly flour, shaking off the excess.

2 large ripe tomatoes

Blanch tomatoes by dropping them into a saucepan of boiling water until skin splits. Peel, seed and julienne tomatoes.

1 tbsp./15 mL. olive oil
1 tbsp./15 g. butter

Sauté veal on both sides in hot oil in an ovenproof skillet on medium heat for 2 minutes per side until golden brown.

Put tomatoes on top of veal in skillet.

salt (to taste)
freshly ground black pepper (to taste)

Season with salt and pepper.

4 oz./125 g. Mozzarella cheese, thinly sliced

Cover veal and tomatoes with slices of Mozzarella cheese.

Put skillet in oven and bake at 400° F/200° C until cheese melts.

Sauce:

2/3 cup/150 mL. veal stock
(see p. 31)
1/4 cup/50 mL. dry red wine
1/2 cup/125 mL. tomato sauce
(see p. 33)

Mix veal stock, wine and tomato sauce together in another skillet and bring to a boil on high heat, then reduce by simmering on medium heat for 5 minutes until sauce thickens.

salt (to taste)
freshly ground black pepper (to taste)

Season with salt and pepper.

Put veal on a warm serving platter or on warm plates.
Coat with sauce and serve.

This recipe for Vitello Umberto di Savoia serves 2 people. Vitello Umberto di Savoia is illustrated on p. 157.

BISTECCHINA DI VITELLO
Veal Chops with Capers

2 (8 oz./250 g.) veal chops
salt (to taste)
freshly ground black pepper (to taste)
1 tsp./5 g. Dijon mustard

Pound veal lightly to flatten it.
Rub veal with mustard, then season veal with salt and pepper.

2 tbsp./30 mL. olive oil
2 tbsp./30 g. butter

Sear veal in hot oil and butter in a skillet on high heat, then sauté on high heat for 3-4 minutes per side (for medium rare meat).
Remove veal from skillet and keep warm.

Sauce:

1/2 cup/125 mL. dry white wine
juice of 1/2 lemon

Deglaze skillet with wine and lemon juice.

2 tbsp./30 g. butter
1 tbsp./15 mL. capers, drained

Add butter and capers to wine and lemon juice, stir until well blended, careful not to mash the capers, and reduce by one-half by simmering on medium heat.

Put veal on a warm serving platter or on warm plates.
Coat with sauce and serve.

This recipe for Bistecchina di Vitello serves 2 people. Bistecchina di Vitello is illustrated on p. 157.

LOMBATINA DI VITELLO PIZZAIOLA
Veal Chops with Tomatoes and Herbs

2 (8 oz./250 g.) veal chops	*Pound veal lightly to flatten it.*
olive oil	*Cover the bottom of a skillet in oil and sauté veal in hot oil on high heat until done as desired.* *Do not sauté for more than 4 minutes per side.*

Sauce:

1/3 cup/75 mL. olive oil 1/2 tsp./2 g. garlic, finely chopped	*Sauté garlic in oil in another skillet on medium heat, careful not to burn the garlic.*
1 (12 oz./350 mL.) can of peeled Italian tomatoes	*Add tomatoes to garlic and bring to a boil on high heat, chopping tomatoes with a wooden or stainless steel spoon, then simmer, uncovered, on medium heat for 15 minutes.*
salt (to taste) freshly ground black pepper (to taste)	*Season with salt and pepper.*
1/2 tsp./2 g. fresh oregano, finely chopped 1/4 tsp./1 g. fresh basil, finely chopped	*Season with oregano and basil at the last minute.*
1 tsp./5 g. fresh parsley, finely chopped	*Put veal on a warm serving platter or on warm plates.* *Coat with sauce, sprinkle with parsley and serve.*

This recipe for Lombatina di Vitello Pizzaiola serves 2 people.

SPEZZATINO DI VITELLO
Veal Stew

3 lb./1.5 kg. veal shoulder, cubed 1 1/2-2 inches/4-5 cm. square	*Put veal in a pot.*
2 quarts/2 L. veal stock (*see p. 31*) or cold water	*Add veal stock or water to pot and bring to a boil on high heat, then remove from heat and strain into a bowl through a sieve, separating the veal from the veal stock or water.* *Set veal and veal stock or water aside.*
1/4 cup/50 g. butter 2 tbsp./30 g. flour	*Mix butter and flour together in pot on medium heat, stirring constantly, to make a roux.*
1 medium onion, diced large 1 medium carrot, diced large 1 stalk celery, diced large	*Add onion, carrot and celery to roux and sauté on medium heat for 2-3 minutes.*
1/4 cup/50 mL. dry white wine	*Add veal, veal stock or water and wine to roux, onion, carrot and celery, stir until well blended and simmer on low heat for 45 minutes, stirring frequently.*
1/4 cup/50 mL. whipping cream	*Add cream to roux, onion, carrot, celery, veal, veal stock or water and wine, stir until well blended and simmer on low heat for another 15 minutes.*
salt (to taste) white pepper (to taste)	*Season with salt and pepper.*
12 mushroom caps	*Blanch mushroom caps by dropping them into a saucepan of boiling water for 15 seconds.*
2 tsp./10 g. fresh parsley, finely chopped	*Put veal stew in a warm serving bowl or on warm plates.* *Garnish with blanched mushroom caps, sprinkle with parsley and serve.*

This recipe for Spezzatino di Vitello serves 6 people. Serve on a bed of hot buttered noodles, risotto (see p. 178) or new potatoes.

Illustration #13: Meat, Fowl & Game. *From left to right:* Bistecchina di Vitello (*upper plate*), Vitello Umberto di Savoia (*lower plate*) and Girello Arrosto. Plates courtesy of Holt Renfrew.

GIRELLO ARROSTO
Roast Veal Stuffed with Spinach

Pre-heat oven to 400° F/200° C.

2 (6 oz./175 g.) veal loins, cut into scallops 1/2 inch/1 cm. thick
salt (to taste)
freshly ground black pepper (to taste)

Pound veal lightly to flatten it.
Season veal with salt and pepper.

Stuffing:

1 bunch of fresh spinach

Wash and stem spinach.
Discard any limp or discoloured leaves.

3/4 cup/175 mL. cold water

Steam spinach in boiling water in a covered saucepan for 3-4 minutes, then drain and rinse with cold running water. Remove all water from spinach by squeezing spinach by hand, then dry with a clean cloth. Finely chop spinach and put in a bowl.

1 egg
1 tsp./5 g. Dijon mustard
1 clove garlic, finely chopped
2 tsp./10 g. Parmesan cheese, coarsely grated
salt (to taste)
freshly ground black pepper (to taste)

Beat egg in another bowl, then add mustard, garlic, Parmesan cheese, salt and pepper and mix together.

Add egg, mustard, garlic, Parmesan cheese, salt and pepper to spinach in bowl and mix together thoroughly.
Put stuffing in the centre of each veal scallop and roll up.

2 tbsp./30 g. flour

Lightly flour veal, shaking off the excess.

olive oil

Cover the bottom of a skillet in oil and sauté veal and spinach in hot oil, seam side down, on high heat to make the seam adhere.

Put veal in a casserole dish and put casserole dish in oven and bake at 400° F/200° C for 7 minutes.

Sauce:

2/3 cup/150 mL. veal stock (see p. 31)
1/4 cup/50 mL. port wine

Mix veal stock and wine together in skillet and bring to a boil on high heat, then reduce by simmering on medium heat for 5 minutes until sauce thickens (cont'd over).

Cont'd from page 159

1/4 cup/50 g. butter	Add butter to veal stock and wine and stir until well blended.
salt (to taste) freshly ground black pepper (to taste)	Season with salt and pepper.
	Put veal on a warm serving platter or on warm plates. Coat with sauce and serve.

ARROSTO DI VITELLO CON SALSA DI FUNGHI
Roast Loin of Veal with Mushroom Sauce

	Pre-heat oven to 450° F/230° C.
3 lb./1.5 kg. veal loin roast olive oil salt (to taste) freshly ground black pepper (to taste) 1 clove garlic, cut in slivers	Rub veal with oil. Season veal with salt and pepper and using the edge of a sharp knife, insert slivers of garlic into the surface of the veal.
	Put veal in a shallow roasting pan and put roasting pan in oven and roast at 450° F/230° C for 10 minutes, then reduce heat and roast at 350° F/180° C for 1 hour (20 minutes per pound/ 40 minutes per kilogram).

Mushroom Sauce:

1 tsp./5 mL. olive oil 1 tsp./5 g. butter 1 cup/250 g. mushrooms, thinly sliced	Sauté mushrooms in oil and butter in a skillet on medium heat for 3 minutes until brown.
1/4 cup/50 mL. dry white wine	Add wine and the veal juices from roasting pan to mushrooms and stir until well blended.
1 cup/250 mL. whipping cream	Add cream to mushrooms, wine and veal juices, stir until well blended and reduce by simmering on medium heat until sauce thickens slightly.
salt (to taste) freshly ground black pepper (to taste)	Season with salt and pepper.
2 tsp./10 g. fresh parsley, finely chopped	Put veal on a warm serving platter and carve into slices 1/2 inch/1 cm. thick. Put veal slices on warm plates. Spoon sauce over veal, sprinkle with parsley and serve.

OSSO BUCO
Braised Veal Shank

Pre-heat oven to 350° F/180° C.

6 veal shin bones,
well covered in meat
salt (to taste)
freshly ground black pepper (to taste)
1/4 cup/50 g. flour

Season veal with salt and pepper.
Dip veal in flour, shaking off the excess.

1/4 cup/50 mL. olive oil
or vegetable oil

Sauté veal on all sides in hot oil in a
large skillet on medium heat until brown
to seal in the meat's juices.

Put veal in a casserole dish just big enough
to contain the meat.

Sauce:

1 tsp./5 mL. olive oil
1 tsp./5 g. butter
1 large onion, finely chopped

Sauté onion in oil and butter in another
skillet on medium heat until onion is
transparent.

1 medium carrot, finely chopped
1 stalk celery, finely chopped
2 cloves garlic, finely chopped

Add carrot, celery and garlic to onion
and sauté on medium heat for 5 minutes.

1 cup/250 mL. dry red wine
1 (32 oz./900 mL.) can of peeled Italian
tomatoes, finely chopped,
or equivalent fresh tomatoes,
and their liquid
1 tsp./5 g. brown sugar

Add wine, tomatoes and their liquid and
brown sugar to onion, carrots, celery and
garlic and stir until well blended.

salt (to taste)
freshly ground black pepper (to taste)

Season with salt and pepper.

Cover veal with sauce and put casserole
dish, covered, in oven and bake at
350° F/180° C for 1 1/2 hours.
Bake uncovered for the last 1/2 hour.

gremolata (*see below*)

Put veal on a warm serving platter
or on warm plates.
Sprinkle with gremolata and serve.

Gremolata:

2 tsp./10 g. lemon peel, grated
1 clove garlic, finely chopped
4 tsp./20 g. fresh parsley,
finely chopped

Mix lemon peel, garlic and parsley
together in a bowl.

This recipe for Osso Buco serves 6 people. Osso Buco is illustrated on p. 158. The recipe
for Girello Arrosto on pp. 159-160 serves 2 people. Girello Arrosto is illustrated on
p. 157. The recipe for Arrosto di Vitello con Salsa di Funghi on p. 160 serves 2 people.

VITELLO TONNATO
Cold Veal with Tuna Sauce

3 1/2 lb./1.75 kg. boneless leg of veal, rolled

Put veal in a Dutch oven or heavy pot.

1 onion, quartered
1 large carrot, coarsely chopped
2 stalks celery and celery top, coarsely chopped
2 cups/450 mL. dry white wine
juice of 1 lemon
peel of 1 lemon (just the peel, not the white part)
1 bayleaf
1/4 cup/50 mL. oil

Add onion, carrot, celery, wine, lemon juice, lemon peel, bayleaf and oil to veal in Dutch oven or pot.

4 cups/900 mL. cold water

Add water to veal, onion, carrot, celery, wine, lemon juice, lemon peel, bayleaf and oil, cover pot and bring to a boil on high heat, then simmer on low heat for 1 1/2-2 hours until veal is tender.

Remove veal from pot and strain cooking liquid into another pot through a sieve lined with a linen or muslin cloth; discard vegetables and herbs.

Put veal back into strained cooking liquid and allow veal to cool in liquid.

When veal is cooled, drain veal and put on a serving platter; reduce cooking liquid by three-quarters on high heat.

Tuna Sauce:

3 (6.5 oz./184 g.) tins of tuna, packed in oil
2 (2 oz./50 g.) tins of anchovy fillets, drained and washed

Mix tuna and anchovy fillets together in a bowl and pound to form a paste.

Add a few tablespoons of the reduced cooking liquid to pounded tuna and anchovy fillets and mix together thoroughly.

3 cups/700 mL. mayonnaise
(see p. 163)

Add tuna and anchovy mixture to mayonnaise a little at a time and stir until well blended.

1 (3 1/2 oz./99 mL.) jar of capers, drained
4-5 gherkins
1 lemon, cut in slices

Put veal on a serving platter and carve into slices.
Lightly coat veal slices with tuna sauce.
Sprinkle capers and gherkins on top of tuna sauce, then put lemon slices around the edge of the serving platter and serve.

Mayonnaise:

All ingredients must be at room temperature. Eggs and oil will not emulsify if they are cold and the mayonnaise will not thicken if ingredients are too warm.

4 egg yolks

Using a fork, break up egg yolks in a bowl.

1/2 tsp./2 g. salt
1/8 tsp./pinch of white pepper
1 tbsp./15 mL. white vinegar or lemon juice

Add salt, pepper and only a few drops of vinegar or lemon juice to egg yolks and stir until well blended.

3 cups/700 mL. oil

Add oil very slowly, by droplets from a spoon, to egg yolks and whisk quickly and smoothly in the same direction with a thin wire whisk.
Stop adding oil if traces of oil appear on the surface of the mixture and proceed only when all the oil has been absorbed. After the first few spoonfuls of oil, the mayonnaise should suddenly become quite thick.
The oil can be added more freely now as the mayonnaise is less likely to separate. Continue to add oil to egg yolks, whisking constantly in the same direction. Alternate oil and vinegar until both are used up.
If the mayonnaise separates, it can be rescued by breaking an egg yolk in another bowl and adding separated mayonnaise to egg yolk and whisking constantly.

This recipe for Vitello Tonnato serves 6-8 people. Serve it chilled or at room temperature. The mayonnaise recipe yields approximately 3 cups/700 mL.. In making the mayonnaise recipe, for meat and fish, use part mild olive oil, part vegetable oil; for salads or in the Rigatoni dell' Ortolano recipe, use vegetable oil, such as corn oil or safflower oil.

FILETTO DI BUE AL BAROLO
Medallions of Beef with Barolo Wine Sauce

4 (4 oz./125 g.) fillets of beef, cut into medallions 1 1/2 inches/4 cm. thick
salt (to taste)
freshly ground black pepper (to taste)
1/4 cup/50 mL. vegetable oil

Press beef with the palm of your hand to slightly flatten it.
Season beef with salt and pepper, then brush with oil (or marinate beef for a few hours in oil that has been seasoned with salt, pepper and garlic).

Marinade (optional):

2 cups/450 mL. vegetable oil
salt (to taste)
freshly ground black pepper (to taste)
2 cloves garlic, finely chopped

vegetable oil

Coat the bottom of a skillet in oil, then sauté beef in hot oil on high heat until done as desired.
Remove beef from skillet and keep warm; discard excess oil from skillet.

Barolo Wine Sauce:

1/4 cup/50 mL. full-bodied dry red wine (Barolo)

Deglaze skillet with wine.

1/4 cup/50 mL. veal stock (see p. 31)

Add veal stock to wine and reduce by simmering on medium heat for 2-3 minutes until sauce thickens.

1 tsp./5 g. butter

Add butter to wine and veal stock and stir until well blended.

salt (to taste)
freshly ground black pepper (to taste)

Season with salt and pepper.

Put beef on a warm serving platter or on warm plates.
Coat with sauce and serve.

This recipe for Filetto di Bue al Barolo serves 2 people.

BISTECCA ALLA CREMA
Cubed Beef in Cream

12-16 oz./350-450 g. fillet of beef,
diced 1 inch/2.5 cm. square

1 tbsp./15 mL. olive oil 1 tbsp./15 g. butter 1 small onion, finely chopped	*Sauté onion in oil and butter in a skillet on medium heat until onion is transparent.*
	Add cubed beef to onion and sauté on medium heat for 4-5 minutes (or longer if you prefer).
salt (to taste) freshly ground black pepper (to taste)	*Season with salt and pepper.*
	Leave beef in skillet.

Sauce:

2 tbsp./30 mL. cognac	*Add cognac to onion and beef and flambé for 15-20 seconds.*
1/4 cup/50 mL. beef consommé (see p. 20)	*Douse flame with beef consommé and reduce by simmering on medium heat for 2-3 minutes.*
1/2 cup/125 mL. whipping cream	*Add cream to onion, beef, cognac and beef consommé, stir until well blended and cook on medium heat for 3-4 minutes until sauce thickens slightly.*
2 tsp./10 g. fresh parsley, finely chopped	*Put beef on a warm serving platter or on warm plates. Coat with sauce, sprinkle with parsley and serve.*

This recipe for Bistecca alla Crema serves 2 people. Serve with hot buttered noodles.

BISTECCA ALLA FIORENTINA
Marinated Porterhouse Steak

1 (2 lb./1 kg.) Porterhouse steak
salt (to taste)
freshly ground black pepper (to taste)

*Season steak heavily with salt and pepper.
Use more salt and pepper than you
normally would use.*

Marinade:

2 tbsp./30 mL. dry red wine
juice of 1/2 lemon
2 cloves garlic, finely chopped

*Mix wine, lemon juice and garlic together
in a bowl.*

1 cup/250 mL. olive oil

*Slowly add oil in a steady stream to wine,
lemon juice and garlic and whisk
constantly in the same direction
until oil is well blended.*

*Put steak in a shallow glass or ceramic
dish just big enough to hold it and pour
marinade over steak.
Refrigerate for at least 12 hours,
occasionally turning steak over.*

*This recipe is best when cooked on a
barbecue, but it can be pan fried.*

olive oil

*To pan fry: coat the bottom of a skillet
with oil, sear steak on both sides in hot oil
on high heat, then sauté on medium heat
until done as desired.*

1/2 lemon, cut in wedges

*Carve meat from the bone, cutting
steak in two.
Put steak on warm plates, garnish with
lemon wedges and serve.*

This recipe for Bistecca alla Fiorentina serves 2 people.

BISTECCA ALLA TARTARA
Steak Tartare

1 lb./450 g. fillet of beef

Trim excess fat and tissue from beef and chop or grind coarsely in a food processor. Do not make a paste.

1 clove garlic
salt (to taste)
freshly ground black pepper (to taste)

Mash garlic in a wooden bowl, then add salt and pepper and mix together.

3 dashes of Worcestershire sauce
1 dash of tabasco sauce
2 tbsp./30 mL. brandy
juice of 1/2 lemon
1/2 tsp./2 g. Dijon mustard

Add Worcestershire sauce, tabasco sauce, brandy, lemon juice and mustard to garlic, salt and pepper and mix together.

Add chopped beef to garlic, salt, pepper, Worcestershire sauce, tabasco sauce, brandy, lemon juice and mustard and mix together thoroughly.

2 egg yolks
1 tbsp./15 g. onion,
finely chopped
1 tbsp./15 g. fresh parsley,
finely chopped
1 tbsp./15 mL. capers, drained

Beat egg yolks in a bowl, then add onion, parsley and capers and mix together.

Add egg yolks, onion, parsley and capers to garlic, Worcestershire sauce, tabasco sauce, brandy, lemon juice, mustard and chopped beef and mix together thoroughly, careful not to mash the capers.

Mold to a form on a serving platter or on plates and serve.

This recipe for Bistecca alla Tartara serves 6 people. Serve this recipe as an appetizer.

TOURNEDOS FINANZIERE
Beef Medallions with Sweetbreads and Port Wine

2 (7 oz./200 g.) fillets of beef, cut 1 inch/2.5 cm. thick salt (to taste) freshly ground black pepper (to taste)	*Season beef with salt and pepper.*
1 tbsp./15 mL. olive oil 1 tbsp./15 g. butter	*Sauté beef on both sides in hot oil and butter in a skillet on high heat until brown, then sauté on medium heat for 4 minutes per side.* *Remove beef from skillet and keep warm; discard excess oil and butter from skillet.*
4 oz./125 g. calf sweetbreads	*Soak sweetbreads in water for 3-4 hours, then bring to a boil in water, vinegar and lemon juice and drain, peel and slice (see p. 145).*

Sauce:

2 tsp./10 g. butter	*Sauté sweetbreads in butter in another skillet on medium heat for 4-5 minutes until golden brown.*
2 tsp./10 g. shallot, finely chopped	*Add shallot to sweetbreads and sauté on medium heat for 1 minute.*
2 tbsp./30 mL. port wine	*Add wine to sweetbreads and shallot and flambé.*
3/4 cup/175 mL. veal stock (see p. 31)	*Douse flame with veal stock, stir until well blended, then reduce by simmering on medium heat for 4-5 minutes until sauce thickens.*
1/4 cup/50 g. butter	*Add butter to sweetbreads, shallot, wine and veal stock and stir until well blended.*
salt (to taste) freshly ground black pepper (to taste)	*Season with salt and pepper.*
	Put beef on a warm serving platter or on warm plates. *Coat with sauce and serve.*

This recipe for Tournedos Finanziere serves 2 people. Tournedos Finanziere is illustrated on p. 158. The recipe for Steak con Pepe Grosso on p. 169 serves 2 people. The recipe for Spezzatino d' Agnello on p. 169 serves 6 people. Serve with a purée of potato.

STEAK CON PEPE GROSSO
Pepper Steak

2 (8 oz./250 g.) New York steaks 2 tsp./10 g. Dijon mustard 2 tsp./10 g. black peppercorns, coarsely cracked	*Rub steak with mustard.* *Press cracked peppercorns into steak* *so that they adhere to the meat.*
2 tsp./10 mL. olive oil 2 tsp./10 g. butter	*Sauté steaks in hot oil and butter in a* *skillet on high heat for 2-3 minutes* *per side.*
2 tbsp./30 mL. cognac	*Pour cognac into skillet and flambé* *for 10-15 seconds.*
	Remove steaks from skillet and keep *warm.*

Sauce:

1/4 cup/50 mL. beef consommé (*see p. 20*)	*Deglaze skillet with beef consommé,* *stirring in cognac.*
1/4 cup/50 mL. whipping cream	*Add cream to beef consommé and cognac,* *stir until well blended and reduce by* *simmering on medium heat for 2-3 minutes.*
salt (to taste)	*Season with salt only.*
	Put steaks on a warm serving platter *or on warm plates.* *Coat with sauce and serve.*

SPEZZATINO D' AGNELLO
Lamb Stew

3 lbs./1.5 kg. lamb, cubed 2 inches/5 cm. square cold water	*Put lamb in a pot and cover* *with cold water.*
2 cloves garlic, finely chopped 1/8 tsp./pinch of fresh rosemary	*Add garlic and rosemary to lamb in pot,* *bring to a boil on high heat, then simmer* *on low heat for 45 minutes, frequently* *skimming the froth off the top.*
6 baby carrots, diced large 6 baby turnips, diced large 1 leek, washed and diced large	*Add carrots, turnips and leek to lamb,* *garlic and rosemary and simmer on low* *heat for another 20 minutes until* *vegetables are tender.*
salt (to taste) freshly ground black pepper (to taste)	*Season with salt and pepper.*
1 tbsp./15 g. fresh parsley, finely chopped	*Put lamb stew into a warm serving bowl* *or on warm plates.* *Sprinkle with parsley and serve.*

COSTATE D' AGNELLO MARTINI ROSSI
Rack of Lamb with Martini Rossi Sauce

Pre-heat oven to 400° F/200° C.

6 lbs./3 kg. uncleaned rack of lamb
equals 3 lbs./1.5 kg. cleaned
rack of lamb

Trim excess fat off the rack of lamb.
We recommend you have your butcher
do this.

3 tsp./15 g. Dijon mustard

Rub lamb with mustard.

1 1/2 tsp./7 g. salt
1 1/2 tsp./7 g. freshly ground
black pepper
3 tsp./15 g. mixed spice
—fennel seeds and rosemary

Season lamb with salt, pepper and mixed
spice.

olive oil

Sauté lamb in hot oil in a large skillet on
medium heat for 5 minutes until brown
to seal in the meat's juices.

Put lamb in a shallow roasting pan and
put roasting pan in oven and roast at
400° F/200° C for 30 minutes for
medium rare meat.
Remove lamb from roasting pan and keep
warm.

Martini Rossi Sauce:

1/3 cup/75 mL. red sweet vermouth

Deglaze roasting pan with vermouth.

3/4 cup/175 mL. demi-glace
(*see p. 31*)

Add demi-glace to vermouth and reduce
by simmering on medium heat for
5 minutes.

Put lamb on a warm serving platter
and carve into individual chops.
Put lamb chops on warm plates.
Coat with sauce and serve.

This recipe for Costate d' Agnello Martini Rossi serves 6 people. Costate d' Agnello Martini Rossi is illustrated on p. 158. Demi-glace is not necessary for this recipe. The recipe can be completed by adding the vermouth to the lamb while still in the roasting pan and broiling both sides of the lamb until brown and crispy.

COSCIOTTO D' AGNELLO
Roast Leg of Lamb

Pre-heat oven to 400° F/200° C.

1 (3 lb./1.5 kg.) leg of lamb salt (to taste) freshly ground black pepper (to taste) 1 tbsp./15 g. Dijon mustard 2 cloves garlic, cut in slivers 1 tbsp./15 mL. olive oil	*Season lamb heavily with salt and pepper.* *Use more salt and pepper than you* *normally would use.* *Rub lamb with mustard.* *Using the edge of a sharp knife, insert* *slivers of garlic into the surface of the lamb.* *Thinly coat lamb with oil.*
olive oil	*Coat the bottom of a shallow roasting pan* *with oil and put lamb in pan.*
1 large onion, quartered	*Surround lamb with onions.*
2 tsp./10 g. fresh rosemary	*Sprinkle lamb with rosemary.*
	Put roasting pan in oven and roast at *400° F/200° C for 10 minutes, then reduce* *heat to 375° F/190° C and roast* *for 45 minutes for medium rare meat* *(15 minutes per pound/30 minutes* *per kilogram).*
Dijon mustard	*Put lamb on a warm serving platter* *and carve into slices.* *Put lamb slices on warm plates (onion* *can be eaten as well).* *Serve with Dijon mustard on the side.*

This recipe for Cosciotto d' Agnello serves 6 people. Serve with roast potatoes and baby carrots.

COSTOLETTE DI MAIALE CON RAFANO
Pork Chops with Radish Sauce

Pre-heat oven to 375° F/190° C.

2 (6-8 oz./175-250 g.) pork chops
salt (to taste)
freshly ground black pepper (to taste)
1/4 cup/50 g. flour

*Season pork chops with salt and pepper.
Lightly flour, shaking off the excess.*

1 egg

*Beat egg in a bowl, then dip pork chops
in egg.*

1/2 cup/125 g. bread crumbs

*Put bread crumbs in another bowl and
dip pork chops in bread crumbs, pressing
the bread crumbs into the pork chops so
that they adhere.*

1 tbsp./15 mL. olive oil
or vegetable oil
1 tbsp./15 g. butter

*Sauté pork chops on both sides in hot oil
and butter in an ovenproof skillet on
medium heat for 4-5 minutes per side
(depending on thickness).
Do not burn the bread crumbs.*

*Put skillet in oven and bake at
375° F/190° C for 10-12 minutes
or until done.*

Radish Sauce:

1/2 cup/125 mL. whipping cream

*Put cream in another skillet and cook on
medium heat until it begins to bubble.*

1/4 cup/50 g. grated horseradish

*Add horseradish to cream, stir until
well blended and reduce by simmering
on medium heat for 2-3 minutes.*

salt (to taste)
freshly ground black pepper (to taste)

Season with salt and pepper.

2 tsp./10 g. fresh parsley,
finely chopped

*Put pork chops on a warm serving platter
or on warm plates.
Coat with sauce, sprinkle with parsley
and serve.*

*This recipe for Costolette di Maiale con Rafano serves 2 people. The recipe for Maiale
Arrostito on p. 173 serves 6 people.*

MAIALE ARROSTITO
Pork Roast in Herbs and White Wine

Pre-heat oven to 400° F/200° C.

1 (4-5 lb./2-2.5 kg.) pork butt roast, boned and tied
1 tsp./5 g. fresh rosemary
2 tsp./10 g. fresh sage, finely chopped
salt (to taste)
freshly ground black pepper (to taste)
3 cloves garlic, cut in slivers

Rub pork with rosemary and sage.
Season pork with salt and pepper.
Using the edge of a sharp knife, insert slivers of garlic into the surface of the pork.

2 cups/450 mL. dry white wine

Put pork in a roasting pan and pour wine into the bottom of the pan.

2 potatoes, peeled and diced large
1 large onion, diced large
2 medium carrots, diced large
2 stalks celery, diced large

Put roasting pan in oven and roast at 400° F/200° C for 20 minutes, then reduce heat to 325° F/160° C, add vegetables and roast for 2 1/3-3 hours (35 minutes per pound/70 minutes per kilogram), basting pork with pan juices approximately every 10 minutes.
To test: pierce pork with a fork. If juices run clear yellow with no traces of pink, roast is done.
Remove pork from roasting pan and keep warm; strain vegetables and pan juices into a small pot through a sieve, mashing the vegetables in the sieve to get all their juices.
Discard mashed vegetables and put pot with vegetable juices and pan juices on medium heat.

Sauce:

2 tbsp./30 mL. dry white wine

Add wine to vegetable juices and pan juices and stir until well blended.

1 cup/250 mL. whipping cream

Add cream to vegetable juices, pan juices and wine, stir until well blended and cook on medium heat until sauce thickens slightly.

salt (to taste)
freshly ground black pepper (to taste)

Season with salt and pepper.

2 tsp./10 g. fresh parsley, finely chopped

Put pork on a warm serving platter and carve into slices.
Put pork slices on warm plates.
Coat with sauce, sprinkle with parsley and serve.

CAPONATA
Mixed Vegetables in a Casserole

Pre-heat oven to 350° F/180° C.

1/4 cup/50 mL. olive oil
1 small onion, diced large
2 cloves garlic, finely chopped

Sauté onion and garlic in oil in an ovenproof skillet on medium heat until onion is transparent.

1 medium zucchini,
diced 1 inch/2.5 cm. square
1/4 eggplant,
diced 1 inch/2.5 cm. square
2 medium green or red peppers,
diced 1 inch/2.5 cm. square

Add zucchini, eggplant and peppers to onion and garlic and sauté on medium heat for 10 minutes.

2 medium ripe tomatoes

Blanch tomatoes by dropping them into a saucepan of boiling water until skin splits. Peel, seed and chop tomatoes.
Add tomatoes to onion, garlic, zucchini, eggplant and peppers.

salt (to taste)
freshly ground black pepper (to taste)
1 tbsp./15 g. fresh parsley,
finely chopped
1/4 tsp./1 g. fresh oregano,
finely chopped

Season with salt, pepper, parsley and oregano.

Put ovenproof skillet, partly covered, in oven and bake at 350° F/180° C for 10 minutes until vegetables are tender.

Serve hot on warm plates or cold on chilled plates.

This recipe for Caponata serves 2 people. Caponata can be served as an antipasto. Caponata is illustrated on the page opposite.

Illustration #15: Vegetables. *From left to right*: Zucchini in Padella, Melanzane alla Parmigiana and Caponata. Tiles courtesy of World Mosaic Ltd.; plates courtesy of The Patio Gallery.

MELANZANE ALLA PARMIGIANA
Eggplant Parmesan

Pre-heat oven to 350° F/180° C.

1 medium eggplant — *Slice eggplant 1/4 inch/.5 cm. thick.*

Egg Mixture:

1 egg
1 cup/250 mL. half and half cream
5 tbsp./75 g. flour
salt (to taste)
freshly ground black pepper (to taste)

Beat egg in a bowl, then add half and half cream, flour, salt and pepper and mix together.

Dip eggplant slices in egg mixture, letting the excess run off back into the bowl.

vegetable oil — *Cover the bottom of a skillet in oil to a depth of 1/4 inch/.5 cm.*

Fry eggplant on both sides in hot oil in skillet on high heat until crispy and golden. Drain eggplant on a cloth or paper towel.

butter
1 cup/250 mL. white sauce
(see p. 32)
1 cup/250 mL. tomato sauce
(see p. 33)
1/4 cup/50 g. Parmesan cheese,
coarsely grated

Butter the bottom of a casserole dish, then layer with one-third of white sauce, one-third of tomato sauce, half the eggplant and one-third of the Parmesan cheese.
Repeat, ending with the white sauce, tomato sauce and Parmesan cheese on top.

salt (to taste)
freshly ground black pepper (to taste)
1/8 tsp./pinch of fresh oregano,
finely chopped
3 dashes of tabasco sauce
(optional)

Sprinkle salt, pepper and oregano on top of eggplant, white sauce, tomato sauce and Parmesan cheese and add tabasco sauce if you like it spicy.

Put casserole dish in oven and bake at 350° F/180° C for 20 minutes until bubbling and golden.

Serve from casserole dish or put on warm plates and serve.

This recipe for Melanzane alla Parmigiana serves 2 people. Melanzane alla Parmigiana is illustrated on p. 175.

Illustration #16: Desserts & Cheeses. *Left foreground:* Pere al Vino Rosso all' Italiana. *Right foreground:* Banane Sciroppate al Brandy. *On the cheese tray. Across the top:* Parmesan, Asiago, Friulano. *Second row:* Emmenthal and Provoletti. *Third row (with radishes):* Castello, Romano, Bel Paese. *Foreground:* Pecorino Crotonese, Caciotta, Mozzarella and Ricotta. Tiles courtesy of World Mosaic Ltd.

RISOTTO
Italian Style Long Grain Rice

Pre-heat oven to 350° F/180° C.

1 tbsp./15 mL. olive oil
1/2 tbsp./7 g. butter
1 tbsp./15 g. onion,
finely chopped
1 clove garlic, finely chopped

Sauté onion and garlic in oil and butter in a casserole dish on medium heat until onion is transparent.

1 cup/250 g. long grain converted rice

Add rice to onion and garlic and stir until rice has absorbed all the oil and butter.

1 1/2 cups/350 mL. chicken consommé
(*see p. 19*)

Add chicken consommé to onion, garlic and rice and bring to a boil on high heat.

salt (to taste)
freshly ground black pepper (to taste)

Season with salt and pepper.

Put casserole dish, partly covered, in oven and bake at 350° F/180° C for 18-20 minutes.

1 tbsp./15 g. fresh parsley,
finely chopped

Serve from casserole dish or put on warm plates.
Sprinkle with parsley before serving.

This recipe for Risotto serves 2 people.

RISOTTO FRUTTI DI MARE
Italian Style Long Grain Rice with Seafood

Pre-heat oven to 350° F/180° C.

1 tbsp./15 mL. olive oil 1 tbsp./15 g. butter 1 clove garlic, finely chopped	*Sauté garlic in oil and butter in a casserole dish on medium heat until garlic is golden.*
1 tbsp./15 g. onion, finely chopped 1/4 small carrot, thinly sliced 1/4 stalk celery, finely chopped	*Add onion, carrot and celery to garlic and sauté on medium heat until onion is transparent.*
1 small ripe tomato	*Blanch tomato by dropping it into a saucepan of boiling water until skin splits. Peel, seed and dice tomato. Add tomato to garlic, onion, carrot and celery.*
1 cup/250 g. long grain converted rice	*Add rice to garlic, onion, carrot, celery and tomato and stir until rice has absorbed all the oil and butter.*
1 cup/250 mL. fish stock (*see p. 30*) or water 1/2 cup/125 mL. dry white wine	*Add fish stock or water and wine to garlic, onion, carrot, celery, tomato and rice.*
1 dash of tabasco sauce salt (to taste) freshly ground black pepper (to taste) 1/4 tsp./1 g. fresh thyme	*Add tabasco sauce to garlic, onion, carrot, celery, tomato, rice, fish stock or water and wine, then season with salt, pepper and thyme.*
	Put casserole dish, partly covered, in oven and bake at 350° F/180° C for 10 minutes.
4 oz./125 g. fresh shrimp 4 oz./125 g. squid, cleaned (*see p. 100*) and chopped	*Add shrimp and squid to rice in casserole dish and stir.*
	Put casserole dish, partly covered, back in oven and bake at 350° F/180° C for another 8-10 minutes.
2 tbsp./30 g. Parmesan cheese, coarsely grated 1/2 lemon, cut into wedges	*Serve from casserole dish or put on warm plates. Garnish with lemon wedges and sprinkle with parsley before serving.*

This recipe for Risotto Frutti di Mare serves 2 people. You can substitute any fresh fish (salmon, red snapper, scallops, prawns, clams or mussels) for the shrimp and squid.

PEPERONATA
Braised Sweet Peppers

Pre-heat oven to 400° F/200° C.

1 tbsp./30 mL. olive oil
1 medium red pepper, quartered
1 medium green pepper, quartered
1 small onion, diced large

Sauté peppers and onion in oil in a skillet on medium heat for 4-5 minutes.

salt (to taste)
freshly ground black pepper (to taste)

Season with salt and pepper.

Put peppers and onion in a casserole dish.

1 clove garlic, finely chopped

Sprinkle garlic on top of peppers and onion.

1/3 cup/75 mL. tomato sauce
(see p. 33)

Pour tomato sauce over peppers, onion and garlic.

1/4 cup/50 g. Parmesan cheese, coarsely grated

Sprinkle Parmesan cheese on top of peppers, onion, garlic and tomato sauce.

Put casserole dish, uncovered, in oven and bake at 400° F/200° C for 15 minutes.

This recipe for Peperonata serves 2 people. Peperonata can be served as an antipasto.

ZUCCHINI IN PADELLA
Zucchini in Tomato Sauce

1 lb./450 g. zucchini
salt (to taste)
freshly ground black pepper (to taste)
1 cup/250 g. flour

Cut zucchini into 1/2 x 3 inch/1 x 8 cm. sections.
Season with salt and pepper.
Lightly flour, shaking off the excess.

1/4 cup/50 mL. olive oil

Sauté zucchini in oil in a skillet on medium heat until golden brown.
Drain zucchini on a cloth or paper towel.

1/2 cup/125 mL. tomato sauce
(see p. 33), warmed

Put zucchini on a warm serving platter or on warm plates.
Spoon tomato sauce over zucchini and serve.

This recipe for Zucchini in Padella serves 2 people. Zucchini in Padella is illustrated on p. 175.

BANANE SCIROPPATE AL BRANDY
Bananas Flambé

6 bananas	*Peel and slice bananas, cutting them in half, then slicing them in half lengthwise.*
1/4 cup/50 g. butter	*Melt butter in a skillet on high heat.*
1 tsp./5 g. orange peel, cut into very fine strips	*When butter is sizzling, add bananas and orange peel and sauté on high heat for 2-3 minutes until bananas are golden brown.* *Remove bananas from skillet and keep warm.*

Sauce:

juice of 1/2 orange 1 tbsp./15 g. sugar	*Add orange juice and sugar to butter and orange peel in skillet, stir until well blended and simmer on medium heat for approximately 2 minutes.*
1/4 cup/50 mL. brandy 1/4 cup/50 mL. mandarin liqueur or any orange liqueur	*Add brandy and mandarin liqueur or any orange liqueur to butter, orange peel, orange juice and sugar and flambé for 10-15 seconds.*
1 cup/250 mL. whipping cream	*Douse flame with cream, stir until well blended and reduce by simmering on medium heat for 2-3 minutes.*
	Put bananas on dessert plates. *Coat with sauce and serve.*

This recipe for Banane Sciroppate al Brandy serves 6 people. Banane Sciroppate al Brandy is illustrated on p. 176. Serve plain or with Gelato alla Vaniglia (see p. 184).

CRESPELLE ALL' ITALIANA
Italian Crêpes

Crêpe Batter:

1 1/2 cups/350 g. flour 1 tbsp./15 g. sugar 1/8 tsp./pinch of salt	Sift flour, sugar and salt together in a mixing bowl.
3 eggs	Lightly beat eggs, then add to flour, sugar and salt and mix together until you have a paste with no lumps.
2 tbsp./30 g. butter, melted 1 1/2 cups/350 mL. milk	Gradually add melted butter and milk to flour, sugar, salt and eggs, stir until well blended, using a wooden spoon, then cover and refrigerate for at least 2 hours, but no longer than 24 hours.
2 tbsp./30 mL. orange liqueur	Add orange liqueur to crêpe batter just before cooking and stir until well blended. The batter should be the consistency of unwhipped whipping cream. If it is too thick, which it may be after refrigeration, add a little water.
	Crêpes should be cooked in a heavy pan so that the heat is evenly distributed. If you do not have a crêpe pan, use a heavy aluminum pan 5-7 inches/ 12.5-18 cm. in diameter.
vegetable oil	Brush pan with a thin film of vegetable oil and put pan on high heat. Pan is ready when a drop of water thrown into the pan forms a little ball and moves quickly over the surface of the pan. Ladle a thin coating of batter into pan, tilting the pan in all directions so that the batter evenly coats the pan. Cook crêpe in pan until the edges are brown. Flip crêpe and cook the other side. Adjust your heat—crêpes should brown to a golden colour. Repeat until all the batter is used up. Brush pan lightly with a thin film of vegetable oil after every 5-6 crêpes. If batter gets too thick, add a little water. Pile crêpes on a plate on top of each other after cooking.

If all the crêpes are not needed at this time, wrap up and store in the freezer. They will last up to 2 weeks in the freezer. When needed, thaw crêpes and continue recipe from this point.

This recipe for crêpe batter yields 14-18 crêpes.

Sauce:

1/4 cup/50 g. butter	*Melt butter in a skillet on medium heat.*
1/4 cup/50 g. sugar 3 tsp./15 g. orange rind, grated (just the peel, not the white part)	*Add sugar and orange rind to butter, stir until well blended and cook on medium heat until butter and sugar slightly carmelizes.*
juice of 3 oranges	*Squeeze orange juice directly into butter, sugar and orange rind, stir until well blended and cook on medium heat until sauce begins to bubble.*
	Put one crêpe at a time in skillet, turning the crêpe over in the sauce so that it gets a generous coating. *Fold crêpe in half, then in half again —quarter the crêpe.* *Keep crêpe in pan.* *Repeat for each crêpe (allowing 2-3 crêpes per person), piling them on top of each other in pan.*
1/2 cup/125 mL. Galliano liqueur	*Add Galliano liqueur to crêpes in pan and flambé until flames die down.*
1 cup/250 mL. whipping cream, whipped (optional)	*Put crêpes on a serving platter or on warm dessert plates.* *Spoon sauce over crêpes and serve with or without whipped cream.*

This recipe for Crespelle all' Italiana serves 6 people.

GELATO ALLA VANIGLIA
Vanilla Ice Cream

Set freezer control at coldest setting.

2 cups/450 mL. milk
2 cups/450 mL. whipping cream
1 cup/250 g. sugar
1 (4 inch/10 cm.) length of vanilla
bean, split and crushed to a powder

Mix milk, cream, sugar and powdered vanilla bean together in an enamel pot on low heat and bring to the scalding point.

6 egg yolks
1/8 tsp./pinch of salt

Beat egg yolks and salt together in a large bowl until eggs are foamy.

Add scalded milk, cream, sugar and powdered vanilla bean to egg yolks and salt in a bowl, stirring constantly. Pour milk, cream, sugar, powdered vanilla bean, egg yolks and salt back into enamel pot, stirring constantly, and simmer on lowest heat possible until mixture is thick enough to coat the back of a metal spoon.
Strain mixture into another bowl through a sieve and put in the refrigerator and chill.
When mixture is chilled, remove from refrigerator and put in metal (not plastic) ice cube trays that have been thoroughly washed with water, then put in freezer. When mixture is almost frozen, but still mushy in the centre, remove from ice cube trays and put in an ice-cold bowl that has been placed in the centre of a larger bowl that is filled with ice cubes.
Beat mixture with a wire whisk or an electric beater until fluffy, then return mixture to ice cube trays.
Cover ice cube trays with foil and freeze for at least 2 hours.

This recipe for Gelato alla Vaniglia yields 1 quart/1 L. of ice cream. For Gelato di Mandoralo/Almond Ice Cream, toast 1 1/2 cups/375 g. of blanched almonds in oven at 350° F/180° C until golden brown, then coarsely chop and mix with 1/4 cup/50 g. berry sugar and 1/8 tsp./pinch of salt. Add to partially frozen ice cream before beating and continue recipe from there. Other nuts may be substituted for the almonds. For Gelato di Frutta/Preserved or Fresh Fruit Ice Cream, peel and dice small 2 cups/450 g. of fruit (leave raspberries and blueberries whole) and mix with 1 cup/250 g. berry sugar, letting stand for 2 hours or until sugar has dissolved, then refrigerate until thoroughly chilled and add to partially frozen ice cream before beating, and continue recipe from there.

PERE AL VINO ROSSO ALL' ITALIANA
Pears in Red Wine

3 cups/700 mL. dry red wine	*Pour wine into a glass or stainless steel bowl.*
1 cup/250 g. sugar	*Add sugar to wine and stir until sugar dissolves.* *Set aside.*
6 large pears	*Peel and core pears, leaving the stems attached.*
	Put pears in a pot just big enough to contain them.
	Pour wine over pears.
1 tsp./5 g. powdered cinnamon 2 cloves 2 orange slices 2 lemon slices	*Add cinnamon, cloves, orange slices and lemon slices to wine.*
	Partly cover pot and bring wine to a boil on high heat, then simmer on medium heat for 15-20 minutes until pears are tender, frequently turning pears and basting them with wine. *Remove pears from heat and allow them to cool in the pot with wine, cinnamon, cloves, orange slices and lemon slices.*
1 cup/250 mL. whipping cream, whipped	*Put pears in a shallow serving bowl or in rimmed dessert plates.* *Spoon wine mixture over pears and serve with whipped cream.*

This recipe for Pere al Vino Rosso all' Italiana serves 6 people. Pere al Vino Rosso all' Italiana is illustrated on p. 176.

TORTA DI MELE
Fresh Apple Tart

Put all ingredients and utensils in the refrigerator for at least 1 hour before starting.

Pre-heat oven to 375° F/190° C.

Pie Shell:

5 1/2 oz./162 g. butter 1 cup/250 g. flour 2 tbsp./30 g. sugar	Gradually add flour and sugar to butter using a pastry cutter and mix together to form a dough until dough has a granular texture.
1 egg 2 tbsp./30 mL. ice water	Beat egg and ice water together, then gradually add to dough and mix together until dough forms a mass.

Put dough in the refrigerator and let it rest for 5 minutes, then divide dough into 2 equal balls.

butter flour	Butter the bottom of 2 (9 inch/22.5 cm.) pie plates, then lightly dust with flour.
flour	Lightly flour a clean flat work surface and put dough on work surface. Lightly flour a rolling pin and roll out dough in one direction, away from you, not forward and backward. Roll from the centre out and make as even a circle as possible. Use only enough flour on surface of rolling pin to keep the dough from sticking. Roll out dough until it is 1/8 inch/.25 cm. thick. Place dough in a pie plate and press tightly into corners around the bottom. Prick dough all over with a fork. Repeat with second ball of dough.

Put pie plate in oven and bake at 375° F/190° C for 10 minutes.

8 cooking apples	Peel, core and thinly slice apples.

Arrange apple slices in the baked pie shell.

4 eggs 1/2 cup/125 g. sugar 2 1/2 cups/500 mL. whipping cream 1/4 cup/50 mL. brandy	Beat eggs in a bowl, then add sugar, cream and brandy and mix together well, but do not whip.

	Pour cream mixture over apple slices in baked pie shell.
	Put pie shell in oven and bake at 350° F/180° C for 25 minutes.
apple jam	*Allow tart to cool slightly, then glaze with apple jam and serve.*

This recipe for Torta di Mele makes 2 (9 inch/22.5 cm.) pies. This recipe can be made with any other fresh fruit in the place of apples.

MACEDONIA DI FRUTTA FRESCA
Fresh Fruit Salad

1 pineapple 3 oranges 1 small melon 2 apples	*Wash and peel pineapple, oranges, melon and apples, then dice large.*
1/2 cup/125 g. purple or green grapes	*Wash and seed grapes.*
	Put pineapple, oranges, melon, apples and grapes in a glass or ceramic bowl.
1/4 cup/50 mL. brandy or any orange liqueur	*Pour brandy or any orange liqueur over pineapple, oranges, melon, apples and grapes and marinate for 1-2 hours.*
1/2 cup/125 g. almonds (optional)	*Fold almonds into pineapple, oranges, melon, apples, grapes, brandy and orange liqueur before serving.*
	Serve in chilled fruit bowls.

This recipe for Macedonia di Frutta Fresca serves 6 people.

ZUPPA INGLESE, A MODO MIO
Sponge Cake with Fruit, My Way

2 x 9 inch/5 x 22 cm. white sponge cake
2 tbsp./30 mL. raspberry
or strawberry jam

Cut cake into pieces 1-2 inches/2.5-5 cm. square and spread jam on the top and bottom of each piece of cake.

Put pieces of cake into a large glass or ceramic bowl.

1/2 cup/125 g. cooked fruit salad
or equivalent uncooked fresh berries
and/or peaches
1/3 cup/75 mL. sweet sherry

Pour fruit and sherry over pieces of cake and distribute evenly, careful not to crumble cake.

Custard:

4 egg yolks
1/4 cup/50 g. sugar

Beat egg yolks and sugar together in the top half of a double boiler, but do not place over boiling water.

1 tsp./5 mL. vanilla extract
1 1/2 cups/350 mL. milk

Add vanilla extract to milk in a saucepan and scald milk on high heat.

Put egg yolks and sugar in the top half of the double boiler over boiling water and slowly add scalded milk and vanilla extract, stirring constantly.
Stir until custard thickens.

Pour custard over sponge cake, but do not mix in.
Allow custard to cool, then spread evenly.

1 cup/250 mL. whipping cream, whipped
1/4 cup/50 g. almonds, slivered

Pipe whipped cream over top of cake and custard.
Garnish with slivered almonds and refrigerate until serving.
Spoon cake onto dessert plates to serve.

This recipe for Zuppa Inglese, a Modo Mio serves 6 people.

ZABAGLIONE

	All ingredients must be at room temperature.
cold water	*Put water in a saucepan and bring to a boil on high heat.*
3 egg yolks 1/3 cup/75 mL. sweet Marsala wine 2 tbsp./30 mL. dry white wine 1 tbsp./15 g. sugar	*Put egg yolks, Marsala wine, white wine and sugar in a stainless steel bowl and set bowl in the middle of boiling water in saucepan.*
	Slightly tip bowl towards you and beat egg yolks, Marsala wine, white wine and sugar with a thin wire whisk in a backward and forward motion.
	Whisk constantly until egg yolks become light and thicken slightly. *Be careful not to cook the eggs too fast as they will scramble.*
fresh fruit or berries (optional)	*Put fresh fruit or berries in the bottom of sherbet glasses.* *Pour zabaglione into sherbet glasses and serve.*

This recipe for Zabaglione serves 2 people. It can be served hot or cold.

Acknowledgments

CP Air for the travel—and special thanks to Kay Staley.

Todd McIntosh for the make-up.

To the management and staff of Umberto's restaurants—and in particular to: Roger Chrisp, Osvaldo Fabbro, Carlos Mas and Carmen Smeraldo; maître d', Eustasio "Chico" Tejedor, José Jorge O. Bicho and Terry Gordon; and chefs, Larry Jacques, Ron Lammie and Doug Leask.

Tiles courtesy of World Mosaic Ltd.—with thanks to Patricia McLean and special thanks to Clifton Phelps. World Mosaic has stores in Toronto, Montreal and Vancouver.

Plates, serviettes and accessories courtesy of Holt Renfrew, The Patio Gallery and Georg Jensen—with thanks to Mr. H.A. Davey of Holt Renfrew, and very special thanks to Alice Vanier of the China Department of Holt Renfrew; with thanks to Harry and Patricia Bekke of The Patio Gallery; and thanks to Gert and Brigit Petersen of Georg Jensen. Holt Renfrew has stores in Toronto, Montreal, Vancouver, Edmonton, Calgary, Winnipeg, Ottawa, Ste. Foy and Québec City. The Patio Gallery is located at 1490 Hornby Street, Vancouver, B.C. V6Z 1X3. Please write for their free catalogue. Georg Jensen has stores in Toronto, Montreal and Vancouver.

David Robinson would like to thank James Burrows for the Pernod; Zonda Nellis for the sweater; and the following four people, who know why: Constance Brissenden, Thomas Hayes, Karl Siegler and Mary Schendlinger. Thank you Jane Hastings and thanks Mum. And thank you Umberto, Marian and John.